FINANCIAL INSTITUTIONS AND SERVICES

FINANCIAL CRIMES: FRAUD, THEFT AND EMBEZZLEMENT

FINANCIAL INSTITUTIONS AND SERVICES

Additional books in this series can be found on Nova's website under the Series tab.

Additional E-books in this series can be found on Nova's website under the E-books tab.

LAW, CRIME AND LAW ENFORCEMENT

Additional books in this series can be found on Nova's website under the Series tab.

Additional E-books in this series can be found on Nova's website under the E-books tab.

FINANCIAL INSTITUTIONS AND SERVICES

FINANCIAL CRIMES: FRAUD, THEFT AND EMBEZZLEMENT

JONATHAN G. MCDOUGAL
EDITOR

Nova Science Publishers, Inc.
New York

For permission to use material from this book please contact us:
Telephone 631-231-7269; Fax 631-231-8175
Web Site: http://www.novapublishers.com

Additional color graphics may be available in the e-book version of this book.

LIBRARY OF CONGRESS CATALOGING-IN-PUBLICATION DATA

Financial crimes : fraud, theft and embezzlement / editors, Jonathan G. McDougal.
p. cm.
Includes index.
ISBN 978-1-61122-479-5 (hardcover)
1. Financial institutions--Law and legislation--United States. 2. Commercial crimes--United States. 3. Fraud--United States. 4. Theft--United States. 5. Embezzlement--United States. I. McDougal, Jonathan G.
KF974.F558 2010
345.73'0268--dc22
2010041300

Published by Nova Science Publishers, Inc. † New York

CONTENTS

PREFACE

The Federal Bureau of Investigation (FBI) investigates matters relating to fraud, theft, or embezzlement occurring within or against the national and international financial community. These crimes are characterized by deceit, concealment, or violation of trust and are not dependent upon the application or threat of physical force or violence. Such acts are committed by individuals and organizations to obtain personal or business advantage. This book presents and discusses information on a variety of financial crimes

- Chapter 1- The U.S. Secret Service has two missions—criminal investigations and protection. Criminal investigation activities, which have expanded since its inception as a small anti-counterfeiting operation at the end of the Civil War, now encompass financial crimes, identity theft, counterfeiting, computer fraud, and computer-based attacks on the nation's financial, banking, and telecommunications infrastructure, among other areas. Protection activities, which have expanded and evolved since the 1890s, include the safety and security of the President, Vice President, their families, and other identified individuals and locations.

Chapter 2- A check cashing enterprise is a fee-based business that will cash a customer's check without requiring an account relationship. The U.S. check cashing industry underwent a significant expansion in the 1990s. Customers are attracted by the immediate access to funds, availability of service without a bank account, and convenience of extended hours of operation. In general, the industry is viewed as a provider of valuable financial services to an under served market segment.

Chapter 3- Amends the Truth in Lending Act (TILA), with respect to credit card accounts under an open end consumer credit plan, to require a creditor to provide written notice not later than 45 days prior to the effective date of: (1) any increase in an annual percentage rate (APR); and (2) any significant change, as determined by rule of the Federal Reserve Board, in the terms of the cardholder agreement (including an increase in fees or finance charges). Prohibits a creditor from increasing any annual percentage rate (APR) of interest, fee, or finance charge applicable to the existing balance on an open end consumer credit card account unless specified conditions are met. Allows a creditor to increase an APR, fee, or finance charge only if the increase is due solely to: (1) expiration of a specified time period (e.g., promotional period) disclosed clearly and conspicuously to the consumer before commencement of the time period; (2) a change in index not under the creditor's control; (3) payment not received during the 30-day grace period after the due date; or (4) completion of a workout or temporary hardship arrangement, or the consumer's failure to comply with such an arrangement. Prohibits any APR increase relating to such an arrangement from exceeding the APR applicable to the particular category of transactions on the day before the effective date of the arrangement. Prohibits a creditor from changing the terms governing repayment of an outstanding balance; but permits the creditor to provide the obligor with specified repayment methods. Requires a creditor that increases the APR based upon factors including the obligor's credit risk, market conditions, or other factors to: (1) consider changes in such factors in subsequently determining whether to reduce the APR for such obligor; and (2) reduce the APR when a review indicates a reduction. Declares that no increase in any APR, fee, or finance charge, with certain exceptions, shall be effective before the end of the one-year period beginning on the date on which the account is opened. States that, in the case of a promotional rate, no written notice of an increase in the APR shall be effective before the end of a six-month period beginning from the date the promotional rate takes effect

Chapter 4- Financial Stability Improvement Act of 2009 - (Sec. 1000A) Directs the Comptroller General to audit and report to Congress within two years after enactment of this Act on all actions taken by the Board of Governors of the Federal Reserve System (Federal Reserve Board) and the federal reserve banks during the current economic crisis.

Chapter 5- The Federal Bureau of Investigation (FBI) investigates matters relating to fraud, theft, or embezzlement occurring within or against the national and international financial community. These crimes are characterized by deceit, concealment, or violation of trust and are not dependent upon the application or threat of physical force or violence. Such acts are committed by individuals and organizations to obtain personal or business advantage. The FBI focuses its financial crimes investigations on such criminal activities as corporate fraud, securities and commodities fraud, health care fraud, financial institution fraud, mortgage fraud, insurance fraud, mass marketing fraud, and money laundering. These are the identified priority crime problem areas of the Financial Crimes Section (FCS) of the FBI.

In: Financial Crimes: Fraud, Theft...
Editors: Jonathan G. McDougal

ISBN: 978-1-61122-479-5

Chapter 1

THE U.S. SECRET SERVICE: AN EXAMINATION AND ANALYSIS OF ITS EVOLVING MISSIONS

Shawn Reese

SUMMARY

The U.S. Secret Service has two missions—criminal investigations and protection. Criminal investigation activities, which have expanded since its inception as a small anti-counterfeiting operation at the end of the Civil War, now encompass financial crimes, identity theft, counterfeiting, computer fraud, and computer-based attacks on the nation's financial, banking, and telecommunications infrastructure, among other areas. Protection activities, which have expanded and evolved since the 1890s, include the safety and security of the President, Vice President, their families, and other identified individuals and locations.

In March 2003, the U.S. Secret Service was transferred from the Department of the Treasury to the Department of Homeland Security as a distinct entity. Prior to enactment of the Homeland Security Act of 2002 (P.L. 107-296), the U.S. Secret Service had been part of the Treasury Department for over 100 years.

During an April 2008 hearing on the FY2009 budget request for the U.S. Secret Service, Members of Congress raised questions related to the missions and organizational location of the Service, and on December 2, 2009, the House Homeland Security Committee conducted a hearing on and questioned U.S. Secret Service presidential protection operations following a White House security breach. Are the two missions of the Service compatible and how should they be prioritized? Is the Department of Homeland Security the most appropriate organizational and administrative location for the Secret Service? These, and other policy questions, have been raised and addressed at different times by Congress and various administrations during the long history of the Service. Additionally, there has been increased interest in the Service due to the recent inaugural security operations and the protection of President Barack Obama. Some may contend that these and other questions call for renewed attention given the recent increase in demand for the Service's protection function (for example, see P.L. 110-326 enacted by the 110th Congress) and the advent of new technology used in financial crimes.

INTRODUCTION

The U.S. Secret Service (USSS), a distinct entity within the Department of Homeland Security (DHS), has two missions—criminal investigations and protection.[1] Criminal investigation activities encompass financial crimes, identity theft, counterfeiting, computer fraud, and computer-based attacks on the nation's financial, banking, and telecommunications infrastructure. The protection mission is the most prominent of the two, covering the President, Vice President, their families, former Presidents, and major candidates for those offices, along with the White House and the Vice President's residence (through the Service's Uniformed Division). Protective duties of the Service also extend to foreign missions in the District of Columbia and to designated individuals, such as the Homeland Security Secretary and visiting foreign dignitaries. Separate from these specific mandated assignments, USSS is responsible for certain security activities such as National Special Security Events (NSSEs), which included the inaugural ceremony of President Obama,[2] the major party quadrennial national conventions, as well as international conferences and events held in the United States.

Over the past century, USSS's protection mission has received more congressional action than its investigation mission, which was the agency's initial responsibility when it was created in 1865.[3] Congressional action includes the 110th Congress-enacted P.L. 110-326, Former Vice President

Protection Act of 2008, which provided Vice Presidents and their families USSS protection for six months after leaving office; a House committee-conducted hearing in April 2008 on the FY2009 budget request and the issue of the Service's presidential candidate protection;[4] and Congress' enactment of the FY2010 DHS appropriations (P.L. 111-83), in which, in the accompanying conference report, the conferees expressed concern because of the delayed notification Congress received on USSS campaign protection cost overruns and indications from the Service that, in FY2010, it has more protectees than budgeted, which may result in the FY2010 protection mission funding being inadequate. Recently, the House Homeland Security Committee conducted a hearing on USSS presidential protection operations following a White House security breach.[5] Additionally, the Senate passed S. 1510, the United States Secret Service Uniformed Division Modernization Act of 2009, which proposes to address personnel management issues within the USSS Uniformed Division. This chapter frames potential policy questions concerning the Service's mission and organization through an examination of the USSS history and its statutory authorities, mission, and present activities within DHS. Additionally, **Appendix B** provides information on direct assaults on and threats to Presidents, Presidents-Elect, and candidates.

U.S. Secret Service Missions

Since 1865, USSS has evolved into a federal law enforcement agency with statutory authority to conduct criminal investigations and protect specific federal officials, individuals, and sites. Congress transferred USSS to the Department of Homeland Security (DHS) in 2002.[6] Previously, it had been part of the U.S. Department of Treasury, since its inception in 1865.

Investigations

The original mission of the Service was to investigate the counterfeiting of United States currency. This mission has been expanded throughout the agency's history through presidential, departmental, and congressional action.[7] At times, early in the agency's history, Secret Service agents conducted investigations that were not related to financial system crimes. Examples include the investigation of the Ku Klux Klan in the late 1860s and counter-espionage activities in the United States during World War I.[8]

Today, USSS conducts criminal investigations into counterfeiting and financial crimes.[9] Within the investigative mission area is the USSS's forensic services and investigative support unit. USSS forensic services personnel conduct analyses of evidence, some of which includes documents, fingerprints, false identification documents, and credit cards, to assist in USSS investigations.[10] USSS's investigative support is also responsible for developing and implementing a criminal and investigative intelligence program. One of the aspects of this program is the Criminal Research Specialist Program, which provides intelligence analysis related to infra-structure protection, conducts forensic financial analysis, and provides research and analytical support to USSS criminal investigations.[11] Additionally, in 1994, Congress mandated that USSS provide forensic and technical assistance to the National Center for Missing and Exploited Children.[12]

Protection

From protecting President Grover Cleveland in 1894 on a part-time basis to the constant protection of President Obama, the USSS history of protection has been directed by unofficial decisions (such as the protection of President Cleveland) and congressional mandate (such as the protection of major presidential candidates). USSS protection activities have increased over the years, with only one instance of a specified type of protectee being removed from the authorized list.[13]

For the first time, in 2008, USSS protected a spouse of a former President who was also a presidential candidate, and it protected a Vice-President who was not running for his political party's nomination. The following are the current individuals authorized USSS protection in 18 U.S.C. §3056(a):

- President, Vice President, President- and Vice President-elect;[14]
- the immediate families of those listed above;[15]
- former Presidents and their spouses;[16]
- former Presidents' children under the age of 16;
- visiting heads of foreign states or governments;
- distinguished foreign visitors and official United States representatives on special missions abroad;

- major presidential and vice presidential candidates and, within 120 days of the general presidential elections, their spouses;[17] and
- former Vice Presidents, their spouses, and their children under the age of 16.[18]

Similar to the evolution of who has been protected by USSS, protection operations have also evolved. Originally, USSS protection entailed agents being, what could be described as, "bodyguards." Now protection includes not only the presence of agents in close proximity of the protectee, but also advance security surveys of locations to be visited,[19] coordination with state and local enforcement entities, and intelligence analysis of present and future threats. The USSS protection mission uses human resources and physical barriers, technology, and a review of critical infrastructures and their vulnerabilities.[20] Statutes also authorize USSS to conduct such other activities as participating in the planning, coordination, and implementation of security operations at special events of national significance, and providing forensic and investigative assistance involving missing or exploited children.[21]

Table 1. U.S. Secret Service Appropriations all Amounts in Millions $

Programs and Activities	FY2009 Enacted	FY2010 Budget Request	FY2010 House-Passed	FY2010 Senate-Passed	FY2010 Enacted
Protection of persons and facilities	806[a]	756	756	760	756
Protective intelligence activities	60	68	68	68	68
National Special Security Events	1	1	1	1	1
Candidate nominee protection	41	0	0	0	0
White House mail screening	34	25	22	22	22
Management and administration	182	221	200	221	221

Table 1. (Continued)

Programs and Activities	FY2009 Enacted	FY2010 Budget Request	FY2010 House-Passed	FY2010 Senate-Passed	FY2010 Enacted
Rowley Training Center	53	54	54	54	54
Domestic field operations	242	261	261	261	261
International field operations	30	31	31	31	31
Electronic crimes program	52	57	57	57	57
Forensic support to the National Center for Missing and Exploited Children	8	8	8	8	8
Acquisition, construction, and improvements	4	4	4	4	4
Uniformed Division modernization	0	4	0	0	0[b]
Total	**1,513**	**1,490**	**1,461**	**1,487**	**1,483**

Source: CRS Analysis of the *FY2010 DHS Congressional Budget Justifications*, the *FY2010 DHS Budget in Brief,* House-reported H.R. 2892 and H.Rept. 111-157, Senate-reported S. 1298 and S.Rept. 111-31, and P.L. 111-83.

Notes:

a. This amount includes the $100 million appropriated for protection of persons and facilities in P.L. 111-8, the FY2009 omnibus.

b. Conferees stated, in the conference report accompanying the FY2010 DHS appropriations act, that there is no funding for Uniformed Division modernization because there are other bills that address this issue (S. 1510). The conferees also state that they support actions to modernize the Uniformed Division.

In recent years Congress has appropriated approximately $1.4 billion annually for the USSS. The following table provides the Service's FY2008-FY2010 appropriations.

Historical Overview of USSS Statutes

The "Investigation Mission" and "Protection Mission" have distinctive characteristics and histories, and each has been affected by unofficial decisions and congressional action. However, its protective mission has received the most congressional attention through legislative action, and has been reinforced by the Service's transfer to DHS following the terrorist attacks on September 11, 2001.[22] Nonetheless, the investigation mission also has expanded. These missions are addressed below.

It should be noted that since USSS's transfer to DHS, any statute still in effect authorizing or requiring the Treasury Secretary to perform some function connected to the USSS's previous statutory responsibilities has now been assumed by the DHS Secretary. This chapter does not detail every law enacted that has affected USSS, but instead attempts to identify important congressional actions that addressed the role and responsibility of the Service. Additionally, **Appendix B** in this chapter provides a list and brief description of the statutes identified in this chapter.

Investigation Mission

In 1806, Congress passed the Enforcement of Counterfeiting Prevention Act, which enabled U.S. marshals and district attorneys to investigate and prosecute counterfeiters.[23] The authority to investigate counterfeiting was later transferred to the Department of Treasury (TREAS) in 1860.[24] In order to regulate U.S. currency and increase sanctions against counterfeiters, Congress passed the National Currency Act in 1863.[25] Also in 1863, the Treasury Secretary directed the Office of the Solicitor of Treasury to assume the department's role in investigating counterfeiting.[26]

Counterfeiting continued to be a problem for the federal government throughout the Civil War; and by 1865, between one-third and one-half of all U.S. currency in circulation was counterfeit.[27] As a result of this currency crisis, the Treasury Secretary established the Secret Service Division (SSD), within the Office of the Solicitor of Treasury in 1865.[28] At the July 5, 1865, swearing in of the new chief of the SSD, William P. Wood, Treasury Secretary Hugh McCulloch stated "your main objective is to restore public confidence in the money of the country."[29] SSD's primary responsibility was to investigate counterfeiting, forging, and the altering of United States' currency and securities.[30]

The Office of Solicitor of the Treasury administered the SSD until 1879.[31] Statutory recognition was given to SSD in 1882 when the 47th Congress appropriated funds, as follows.

> SECRET SERVICE DIVISION.—For one chief, three thousand five hundred dollars; one chief clerk, two thousand dollars; one clerk of class four; two clerks of class two; one clerk of class one; one clerk at one thousand dollars; and one attendant at six hundred and eighty dollars; in all, twelve thousand nine hundred and eighty dollars;[32]

The investigation of counterfeiting continued to be the Service's only mission until 1894, when it acquired its protection function.[33]

In 1915, President Woodrow Wilson directed the Treasury Secretary to have SSD investigate espionage in the United States, which expanded on its limited espionage mission conducted during the Spanish-American War in 1898.[34] This mission was phased out at the end of World War I, similar to its espionage mission ending following the Spanish-American War.

In the first half of the 20th Century, Congress continued to authorize the Treasury Secretary to "direct and use" SSD to "detect, arrest, and deliver into custody of the United States marshal having jurisdiction any person or persons violating" counterfeit laws.[35] In 1948, SSD was also authorized to investigate crimes against the Federal Deposit Insurance Corporation, federal land banks, joint-stock land banks, and national farm loan associations.[36] As throughout USSS's history, Congress continued to amend the Service's investigation mission.[37]

Due to the increased use of computers and electronic devices in financial crime, Congress, in 1984, authorized USSS to investigate violations related to credit card and computer fraud.[38] Two years later in 1986, the Treasury Police Force was merged into the Secret Service Uniformed Division as part of its protection mission.[39]

In the 1990s, Congress continued to amend laws affecting the investigation, prosecution, and punishment of crimes against United States financial systems. One authorized USSS investigation of crimes against financial systems by authorizing the Service to conduct civil or criminal investigations of federally insured financial institutions. This investigation jurisdiction was concurrent with the Department of Justice's investigation authority.[40] Another law was the Violent Crime Control and Law Enforcement

Act of 1994 (P.L. 103-322), which made international manufacturing, trafficking, and possessing of United States currency a crime as if it were committed in the United States. Congress also enacted laws related to telemarketing fraud (P.L. 105-184), and identity theft (P.L. 105-318). Both telemarketing and identity theft are used in committing financial fraud and crime.

Following the terrorist attacks of September 11, 2001, Congress enacted the USA PATRIOT Act.[41] Among numerous provisions addressing the protection of the United States financial systems and electronic device crimes, the act contains a provision that authorizes the Service to establish nationwide electronic crime task forces to assist law enforcement, private sector, and academic entities in detecting and suppressing computer-based crimes.[42] .

Protection Mission

In 1894, SSD began (unofficially) to protect President Grover Cleveland on a part-time basis. In fact, USSS agents guarded him and his family at their vacation home in the Summer of 1894.[43] President William McKinley also received SSD protection during the Spanish-American War and limited protection following the end of the war.[44] There were three SSD agents present when President McKinley was assassinated in Buffalo, New York, but reportedly not fully in charge of the protection mission.[45]

Following the assassination of President McKinley, in 1901, Congress informally requested SSD to protect the President.[46] Five years later Congress, for the first time, appropriated funds for the protection of the President with the passage of the Sundry Civil Expenses Act for 1907 (enacted in 1906).[47]

Even as the SSD's protection mission was authorized by Congress through statute, the Service continued to investigate counterfeiting. Additionally, as with its investigation into the Ku Klux Klan, SSD began another task outside the purview of its original mandate; the investigation of land fraud in the western United States in the early 1900s.[48]

In 1908, SSD's protection mission was expanded to include the President-elect.[49] In that same year, President Theodore Roosevelt transferred a number of SSD agents to the Department of Justice, which served as the foundation for the Federal Bureau of Investigation.[50] Annual congressional authorization of the mandate to protect the President and President-elect began in 1913.[51]

During World War I threats began to arrive at the White House, which resulted in a 1917 law making it a crime to threaten the President.[52]

Additionally, in that same year, Congress authorized SSD to protect the President's immediate family.[53]

As part of increasing the protection of the President and the President's family, the White House Police Force was created in 1922 to secure and patrol the Executive Mansion and grounds in Washington, DC. Initially, the White House Police Force was not supervised or administered by SSD; instead, the President or his appointed representative supervised the White House Police Force.[54] In 1930, however, Congress mandated that the White House Police Force be supervised by the SSD.[55] In 1943, Congress appropriated funding, for the first time, for both the investigation and protection mission, specifically for: "suppressing" counterfeiting and "other" crimes; protecting the President, the President-elect, and their immediate families; and providing funding for the White House Police Force.[56]

In 1951, Congress permanently authorized the "U.S. Secret Service" to protect the President, his immediate family, the President-elect, and the Vice President—if the Vice President so desired.[57] In 1954, Congress used the title "U.S. Secret Service" in an appropriation act.[58]

Eleven years after permanently authorizing USSS's protection mission, Congress called for the protection of the Vice President[59] (or the next officer to succeed the President), the Vice President-elect, and each former President "at his request" for "a reasonable period after he leaves office."[60] In 1963, following the assassination of President John F. Kennedy, Congress enacted legislation that authorized protection for Mrs. Jacqueline Kennedy and her children for two years.[61]

In 1965, Congress authorized permanent protection for former Presidents and their spouses for the duration of their lives, and protection of their children until age 16.[62] Also in that year, Congress increased USSS law enforcement responsibilities by authorizing the Service's agents to make arrests without warrant for crimes committed in their presence.[63]

The initial protection of Mrs. Kennedy (a widow of a former President) was not extended.[64] Congress, in 1967, authorized protection to former Presidents' widows and minor children until March 1, 1969.[65] This protection became permanent in 1968.[66] USSS's protection mission was furthered expanded in that same year following the assassination of Senator Robert F. Kennedy (a presidential candidate). Congress authorized the Treasury Secretary to determine which presidential and vice presidential candidates should receive USSS protection.[67] An advisory committee was established to assist the Treasury Secretary in determining what candidates could receive protection. The committee included the Speaker of the House of

Representatives, the minority leader of the House of Representatives, the Senate majority and minority leaders, and one additional member selected by the committee.[68]

Following a decade of expanding USSS's protection mission, Congress further amended this mission, and renamed the White House Police Force as the Executive Protection Service (EPS) in 1970. Congress authorized the USSS Director to administer the EPS's protection of

- the Executive Mansion and grounds in the District of Columbia (DC);
- any building with presidential offices;
- the President and immediate family;
- foreign diplomatic missions located in the metropolitan DC area; and
- foreign diplomatic missions located in the United States, its territories, and its possessions—as directed by the President.[69]

EPS was renamed the "Secret Service Uniformed Division" in 1977.[70]

Along with the protection of foreign diplomatic missions, Congress, in 1971, authorized USSS to protect visiting heads of foreign states, and other distinguished foreign visitors—at the direction of the President.[71] Congress also authorized the President to direct the protection of United States' official representatives on special missions abroad.[72] Additionally, in 1971, Congress established criminal penalties for a person who " ... knowingly and willfully obstructs, resists, or interferes with an agent of the United States engaged in the performance ... " of USSS's protection mission.[73]

As Congress increased the authority of the USSS to protect foreign diplomatic missions and visitors, it once again expanded protection, this time in 1975, to include the Vice President's immediate family.[74] Congress further refined the protection mission in the Presidential Protection Assistance Act of 1976 (P.L. 94-524) by regulating the number and types of property to be protected by USSS.[75] Also in 1976, Congress further expanded the list of who was eligible for USSS protection by adding presidential and vice presidential candidate spouses.[76] The "protectee" list was again expanded in 1977, when Congress authorized the USSS to continue to protect specified federal officials and their families.[77]

The list was increased with the addition of former Vice Presidents and their spouses for a period to be determined by the President.[78] Temporary residences of the President and Vice President were designated (as determined by the Treasury Secretary) as property that could be protected if occupied in 1982.[79]

For the first time in 1984, Congress enacted a consolidated list—from earlier statutes—of individuals authorized USSS protection. The statute amended 18 U.S.C. §3056, "Powers, authorities, and duties of United States Secret Service."[80] In 1994, the protection of former Presidents and their spouses was limited to 10 years after the President leaves office.[81]

The list of "protectees" has also been affected by presidential directives. As an example, in 1986, the President directed USSS to protect the spouses of visiting heads of foreign states.[82] Any protectee may decline USSS protection except the President, the Vice President, the President-elect, or the Vice President-elect.[83]

As the federal government began to address terrorist threats at the end of the 1990s, President William J. Clinton issued Presidential Decision Directive 62 (PDD 62)—"Protection Against Unconventional Threats to the Homeland and Americans Overseas" on May 22, 1998.[84] As described by the White House, PDD 62 established a framework for federal department and agency counter-terrorism programs that addressed the issues of terrorist apprehension and prosecution, increased transportation security, enhanced emergency response, and enhanced cyber security. PDD 62 also designated specific federal departments and agencies as the "lead" agencies in the event of terrorist attacks.[85] The Service was designated as the lead agency with the leadership role in the planning, implementation, and coordination of operational security for events of national significance—as designated by the President.

On December 19, 2000, President Clinton signed P.L. 106-544, the Presidential Threat Protection Act of 2000, authorizing the USSS—when directed by the President—to plan, coordinate, and implement security operations at special events of national significance.[86] The special events were entitled National Special Security Events (NSSEs). Some events categorized as NSSEs include presidential inaugurations, major international summits held in the United States, major sporting events, and presidential nominating conventions. Among other actions, this act also established the National Threat Assessment Center (NTAC) within USSS. Congress required NTAC to provide the following assistance to federal, state, and local law enforcement agencies:

- threat assessment training;
- consulting on complex threat assessment cases;
- researching threat assessment and targeted violence;

- promoting standardization of federal, state, and local threat assessments and investigations; and
- other threat assessment activities, as determined by the DHS Secretary.[87]

POLICY QUESTIONS

In light of the historical information presented above on the evolution of the statutory foundation for the USSS and its present budget authority, Congress might wish to consider the following policy questions, among others.

Missions

- Should Congress consider what is the optimum or preferred mission of the USSS and whether the mission should consist of both investigation and protection?
- Is the current allocation of resources, with the majority dedicated to the protection mission, appropriate?

Organization

- Six years after the establishment of DHS, is this department the most appropriate administrative location for the USSS?
- What are the advantages and disadvantages of alternative organizational arrangements, including the transfer of some functions and personnel back to the Treasury Department?

Missions

The two USSS missions—investigation and protection—have evolved over 143 years. Its original and oldest mission, which began in 1865, is its investigation mission. Statutorily, the protection mission did not begin until 1906. In FY2009, however, the protection mission received 60% of the agency's funding and employed approximately 73% of its full-time equivalents (FTE). In FY2009, the protection mission was appropriated approximately $942 million, and the investigation mission was appropriated $324 million.[88] Additionally, according to USSS FY2009 congressional justification, the FY2008 protection mission's FTE is 4,850, compared to the investigation mission's FTE of 1,850.

As described earlier in this chapter, USSS's protection mission employs the majority of the Service's agents and receives a larger share of the agency's resources. Additionally, the majority of congressional action concerning USSS has been related to its protection mission. This difference may be the result of the costs associated with an increase in protecting individuals, events, and facilities. The relevant statutes identify what federal officials are authorized, through statute, USSS protection; the role and responsibilities of the Secret Service Uniform Division; and the Service's role in security for NSSEs.

While Congress has maintained USSS's role in investigating financial crimes, congressional action primarily has addressed, and continues to address the Service's protection mission. An example of this is Congress' enactment of P.L. 110-326, the "Former Vice President Protection Act of 2008," which requires the Service to protect former Vice Presidents, their spouses, and minor children for a period up to six months after leaving office. Another example of congressional interest in the Service's protection mission occurred in the FY2008 Consolidated Appropriations Act, when Congress specifically stated that the USSS could not use any funds to protect any federal department head, except the DHS Secretary, unless the Service is reimbursed.[89]

One could argue, potential terrorist attacks and possible direct assaults have resulted in an increase in the need for the Service's protection activities. The Service's protection mission has increased and become more "urgent" due to the increase in terrorist threats and the expanded arsenal of weapons that terrorists could use in an assassination attempt or attacks on facilities.[90] The USSS transfer from the Treasury Department to DHS indicates this change.

The establishment of a single mission, or a distinct primary and secondary mission, for the USSS is one option for Congress in light of this increased terrorist threat. One argument for this is that the majority of the Service's resources are used for its protection mission, and that Congress has raised the issue of the Service's competing missions of protection and investigation. It can be argued, however, that the Service trains its agents in both investigations and protection with no loss of a protectee in the last 45 years. Some have argued, however, that there needs to be an independent examination of the Service's dual mission to evaluate the effectiveness of USSS's training.[91] If there were an evaluation of the Service's two missions, it might be determined that it is ineffective for the USSS to conduct its protection mission and investigate financial crimes.

Specifically, in 2008, USSS was engaged in an increased protection workload which included protection of major presidential candidates, ensuring security for the 2008 presidential nominating conventions, preparing for the transfer of presidential administrations and the January 2009 inauguration. Congress addressed this issue at a hearing in April 2008 on candidate protection.[92] Members expressed concern with the Service's ability to meet the demands of its dual mission.[93] USSS Director, Mark Sullivan stated, at the hearing, that the Service "initiated" candidate protection approximately 18 months before the general election, the earliest it has ever begun protection.[94] Director Sullivan also stated that the Service employed approximately 1,000 Transportation Security Administration screeners, also within DHS, to augment the Service's uniform division's officers for security screening at campaign functions.[95]

It should be noted that in the conference report accompanying the FY2010 DHS appropriations (P.L. 111-83), the conferees expressed concern over the delayed notification Congress received on USSS campaign cost overruns in FY2009. Additionally, the conferees noted that USSS has indicated that its protective responsibilities in FY2010 will include more protectees than budgeted, which may result in the FY2010 protective mission funding being inadequate. Because of this, the conferees directed the DHS chief financial officer and USSS assistant director for administration to brief the House and Senate Appropriations Committees not later than 30 days after the enactment of P.L. 111-83 on the process the Service will implement in FY2010 to ensure that no protection mission funding shortfall occurs. **Appendix A** provides information on death threats and direct assaults on Presidents.

Organization

As one examines the placement of the Service in DHS following the terrorist attacks of September 11, 2001, it might be useful to examine the missions of the Departments of Treasury and Homeland Security, and the Homeland Security Council's *National Strategy for Homeland Security*.[96]

Department of the Treasury's Mission

The Department of the Treasury's mission is to "Serve the American people and strengthen national security by managing the Government's finances effectively, promoting economic growth and stability, ensuring the safety, soundness, and security of the U.S. and international finance systems."[97] Specifically, the Department of the Treasury is authorized to establish a Financial Crimes Enforcement Network (FinCEN), which would, among other activities, identify possible criminal activity to appropriate law enforcement entities; support criminal financial investigations and prosecutions; determine emerging money laundering and financial crime trends; and support intelligence and counterintelligence activities to protect against international terrorism.[98] The Department of the Treasury also has an Office of Intelligence and Analysis which is responsible for the "receipt, analysis, collation, and dissemination" of foreign intelligence and counterintelligence related to the Department of Treasury's operations and responsibilities.[99] Finally, within the Department of Treasury, there is an Office of Terrorism and Financial Intelligence, whose functions include providing policy, strategic, and operational direction relating to

- combating terrorist financing; and
- combating financial crimes, including money laundering, counterfeiting, and other offenses threatening the integrity of banking and financial systems.[100]

These functions are similar to elements of the USSS investigation mission.

Department of Homeland Security's Mission and National Homeland Security Strategy

DHS's mission statement reads "We will lead the unified national effort to secure America. We will prevent and deter terrorist attacks and protect against and respond to threats and hazards to the nation. We will ensure safe and secure borders, welcome lawful immigrants and visitors, and promote the free flow of commerce."[101] More specifically, certain authorities and responsibilities of the Homeland Security Act address USSS activities. Some involve DHS's mission to prevent terrorist attacks within the U.S.[102] and reduce the nation's vulnerability from terrorist attacks.[103] The focus on terrorism prevention, within a homeland security context, is further reinforced with the October 7, 2007, version of the Homeland Security Council's *National Strategy for Homeland Security*. The strategy's four goals are:

- prevent and disrupt terrorist attacks;

- protect the American people, our critical infrastructure, and key resources;
- respond to and recover from incidents that do occur; and
- continue to strengthen the foundation to ensure our long term success.[104]

Arguably, the authority for the USSS to protect specified categories of individuals listed in 18 U.S.C. 3056(a) (provided earlier in this chapter) and the Service's investigation into financial crimes related to terrorism or terrorist organizations meet DHS's mission and the strategy's goals of preventing and disrupting terrorist attacks. Some past assassination attempts on Presidents, Presidents-elect, and candidates have been terrorist attacks, such as the 1901 assassination of President McKinley by an anarchist and the 1951 assassination attempt on President Harry S Truman by two Puerto Rican nationalists.[105] However, to date, no attempted or successful assassination has been attributed to an individual professing to be a terrorist or being a member of a terrorist organization. It is not unreasonable, however, to associate general terrorist threats with potential dangers to top government officials. In its study, through the National Threat Assessment Center (NTAC), USSS found that "assassins and attackers plan their attacks and are motivated by a wide range of issues."[106] The NTAC study also "suggests" that mental illness is not critical to determining legitimate threats; the ability to develop and execute a plan is a more significant factor.[107] Terrorists are motivated by many issues and ideologies, and have proven to be adept at developing and executing plans.

Also, in the *National Strategy for Homeland Security*, "banking and finance" is listed as a critical infrastructure and key resource.[108] USSS's original mandate to investigate crimes against United States' financial system meets the strategy's goal to protect our critical infrastructure and key resources. DHS's National Protection and Programs Directorate contains an Office for Infrastructure Protection (OIP). OIP is responsible for the "coordinated national effort to reduce risk to our critical infrastructures and key resources (CI/KR) posed by acts of terrorism. In doing so, the department increases the nation's level of preparedness and the ability to respond and quickly recover in the event of an attack, natural disaster, or other emergency."[109] It could be assumed that DHS's responsibility for ensuring the protection of critical infrastructure, which includes banking and finance, supports USSS transfer to DHS. Therefore, it could be argued that the USSS is able to effectively execute its missions as a distinct entity within DHS.

It can also be argued that because of the Department of the Treasury's mission to ensure the nation's financial systems, USSS could execute its investigation of financial crimes mission as one of the department's entities—as it was prior to its transfer to DHS in March 2003. This option might ensure that the lead agency for financial crime investigations was part of the federal government's financial department.

This option would require an evaluation of the Service's history of its protection mission when it was part of the Treasury Department, and if the Service would still be effective in this mission if it was reassigned to the Treasury Department. Again, this was an activity USSS executed as part of the Treasury Department prior to March 2003, however, the Service's protection mission has taken on increased significance since September 11, 2001. This may, arguably, be a reason to maintain USSS's protection mission within DHS. Presently, the Service's practice of training its agents in investigations and protection could impede on this division of USSS between the Departments of Treasury and Homeland Security.

Another example of an agency that could possibly assume the Service's investigation mission is the FBI, which has the mission of protecting and defending the United States against terrorist and foreign intelligence threats, and enforcing the criminal laws of the United States.[110] However, this might be problematic, since investigations of financial crimes was the original mission of the USSS. Additionally, the Service has developed a proficiency in investigating financial crimes that the FBI may not be able to replicate, unless USSS personnel and resources were transferred.

It may be argued that it is necessary for Congress to further debate the question of what is the primary USSS mission in order to determine where the Service can most efficiently execute its mission and be appropriately supported. This evaluation could result in the status quo (USSS as a DHS agency), a separation of USSS missions (financial investigations in the Treasury Department and protection in DHS), or the Service being transferred back to the Department of the Treasury. Another possibility may be establishing the USSS as an independent agency that investigates financial crimes and conducts its protection mission. This would require Service coordination with the Treasury Department during financial crime investigations, and coordination with other governmental entities—such as DHS and the Department of Justice—when USSS is executing its protection mission. One additional course of action could be having the Service transferred to a federal department other than Treasury or DHS, such as the Department of Justice. Regardless of how the Service is organized, it may be necessary to further examine how USSS is funded and if the present procedure of funding adequately meets the Service's needs and organization.

CONCLUSION

From 1865 to the present, USSS has been investigating financial crimes, its only activity for the first three decades, and protecting senior executive branch officials, most notably the President. Recently the Service has increased its efforts in cybersecurity and its protection activities due to certain events, such as the terrorist attacks of September 2001 and the war in Iraq. The missions of the Service have evolved and conformed to presidential, departmental, and congressional requirements. Due to evolving technology and tactics used in crimes—including financial, cyber, terrorism, and attempted assassinations—USSS has had to evolve. As the cost of this law enforcement increases, and the number of protectees increases (at least during presidential campaign election years), the Service is having to continue to balance and fulfill its two missions.

APPENDIX A. PRESIDENTIAL DEATH THREATS AND DIRECT ASSAULTS AGAINST PRESIDENTS[111]

Presidential safety is and has been a concern throughout the nation's history. For example, fears of kidnapping and assassination threats to Abraham Lincoln began with his journey to Washington, DC, for the inauguration in 1861. A much more recent example is the breach of Secret Service security at a White House State Dinner on November 24, 2009, where two uninvited guests gained entry to the event. This resulted in a House Homeland Security Committee hearing on December 3, 2009, where the Director of the Secret Service, Mark J. Sullivan, admitted that the breach was a "human error" by Secret Service personnel manning a security checkpoint.[112]

At the December 3 hearing, Director Sullivan stated that there has been no increase of death threats to President Obama when compared to death threats against Presidents George W. Bush and William J. Clinton even though some media sources have reported otherwise.[113] In 1917, Congress enacted legislation that made it a crime to threaten the President.[114] CRS does not have access to information on presidential death threats due to the security classification of this information. The extent to which Presidents have been threatened or targeted remains a matter of conjecture.

Concern for presidential safety is genuine due to the number of attempted and successful assaults against Presidents. Ten Presidents have been victims of direct assaults by assassins, with four resulting in death. Since the Secret Service started protecting Presidents in 1906, seven assaults have occurred, with only one resulting in death (President John F. Kennedy). The following table provides information on assaults against Presidents who were protected by the Secret Service; it does not include information on assaults against Presidents prior to the Service assuming the responsibility of presidential safety.

Table A-1. Direct Assaults on Presidents Protected by the U.S. Secret Service

Date	President	Location	Assailant and Reason
11/01/1950	Harry S. Truman	Washington, DC	Oscar Collazo and Griseilio Torressola, advocates of Puerto Rican independence
11/22/1963	John F. Kennedy[a]	Dallas, TX	Lee Harvey Oswald, motive unknown
09/05/1975	Gerald R. Ford[b]	Sacramento, CA	Lynette Alice Fromme, member of extremist "Mason Family" and mentally unstable
09/22/1975	Gerald R. Ford	San Francisco, CA	Sara Jane Moore, desired to start a revolution with "the upheaval of needed change"
03/30/1981	Ronald W. Reagan	Washington, DC	John W. Hinkley, Jr., mentally unstable
10/29/1994	William J. Clinton	Washington, DC	Francisco M. Duran, motive unknown
05/10/2005	George W. Bush	Tibilisi, Republic of Georgia	Vladimir Arutyunian, motive unknown

Source: CRS Report RS20821, *Direct Assaults Against Presidents, Presidents-Elect, and Candidates*, by Frederick M. Kaiser

Notes:

a. Only President receiving U.S. Secret Service protection to be killed by an assassin.

b. Only President to be assaulted twice while receiving U.S. Secret Service protection.

APPENDIX B. STATUTES ADDRESSING U.S. SECRET SERVICE ACTIVITIES

Statute	Brief Description	Year
2 Stat. 404	The Enforcement of Counterfeiting Prevention Act passed; authorized U.S. marshals and district attorneys to investigate and prosecute counterfeiters.	1806
12 Stat. 102	Counterfeiting investigation authority transferred to the Department of the Treasury.	1860
12 Stat. 665	National Currency Act passed by Congress.	1863
16 Stat. 162	The Office of the Solicitor of the Treasury transferred to the Department of Justice.	1870
22 Stat. 230	Statutory recognition given to the Secret Service Division (SSD) in an appropriation act.	1882
34 Stat. 708	Congress, for the first time, appropriated funds specifically for the protection of the President.	1906
38 Stat. 23	Beginning of annual authorization for presidential protection.	1913
39 Stat. 919	Congress makes it a crime to threaten the President.	1917
40 Stat. 120	Congress authorizes SSD to protect the President's immediate family.	1917
42 Stat. 841	White House Police Force established.	1922
44 Stat. 918	Treasury Secretary authorized to use SSD to investigate counterfeiting.	1926
46 Stat. 328	Congress authorizes SSD to administer and supervise the White House Police Force.	1930
48 Stat. 178	Congress authorizes SSD to investigate and arrest individuals involved in fraud related to the Federal Deposit Insurance Corporation.	1933
57 Stat. 259-260	Congress, for the first time, appropriates funding for the SSD's investigation and protection missions.	1943
62 Stat. 818	SDD authorized to investigate crimes related to federal banks and loan associations.	1948
65 Stat. 122	Congress permanently authorizes the "U.S. Secret Service" to protect the Presidents, their immediate families, Vice Presidents (if so desired), and the Presidents-elect.	1951
67 Stat. 68	Congress, for the first time, uses the title "U.S. Secret Service" in an appropriation act.	1954

(Continued)

Statute	Brief Description	Year
76 Stat. 809	Congress authorizes reimbursement to USSS for funds used to purchase counterfeit currency.	1962
76 Stat. 956	Congress authorizes permanent protection of the Vice President and former Presidents (as requested) for a "reasonable amount of time."	1962
77 Stat. 348	Congress authorizes USSS protection of Mrs. Jacqueline Kennedy and her minor children for two years following the assassination of President John F. Kennedy.	1963
79 Stat. 791	Congress authorizes permanent protection of former Presidents and their spouses during their lifetime, and their children until age 16.	1965
79 Stat. 890	Congress authorizes USSS agents to make arrests without warrants if crimes are committed in their presence.	1965
81 Stat. 466	Congress extends USSS protection to widows of former Presidents and minor children until March 1, 1969.	1967
82 Stat. 170	Congress authorizes the Treasury Secretary to determine what presidential and vice presidential candidates should receive USSS protection, and establishes an advisory committee to assist the Secretary in this determination.	1968
82 Stat. 1198	Congress permanently authorizes the protection of former Presidents' widows and minor children.	1968
84 Stat. 74-75	Congress renames the White House Police Force the Executive Protection Service (EPS), and authorizes the USSS Director to ensure EPS's protection of different locations and facilities.	1970
84 Stat. 1892	Congress makes it a crime to interfere with USSS agents engaged in a protection mission.	1971
84 Stat. 1941	Congress authorizes USSS protection of visiting heads of foreign states, distinguished foreign visitors, and U.S. officials abroad on special missions.	1971
88 Stat. 1765	Congress extends USSS protection of foreign diplomatic missions and the Vice President's immediate family.	1975
90 Stat. 1239	Congress authorizes protection of presidential and vice presidential candidates' spouses.	1976

(Continued)

Statute	Brief Description	Year
90 Stat. 2475	Congress identifies the number and types of residences and properties to be protected by USSS, such as residences owned by Presidents and Vice Presidents.	1976
91 Stat. 3	Congress authorizes USSS protection to specified federal officials. Repealed in 1984 (98 Stat. 3110).	1977
91 Stat. 1371	EPS is renamed the Secret Service Uniform Division.	1977
94 Stat. 2740	Former Vice Presidents and spouses are authorized USSS protection if directed by the President, but not indefinite protection.	1980
96 Stat. 1451	Temporary presidential and vice presidential residences were designated as property that could be protected when occupied.	1982
98 Stat. 2192	USSS authorized to investigate credit card and computer fraud.	1984
98 Stat. 3110	Congress authorizes a specific list of individuals to be protected by USSS, including the President, Vice President, and their immediate families.	1984
104 Stat. 1427	Congress authorizes USSS to conduct civil and criminal investigations into crimes against federally insured financial institutions.	1990
108 Stat. 2043	Congress mandates that USSS provide technical and analytical assistance to the National Center for Missing and Exploited Children.	1994
108 Stat. 2413	Congress modifies authorities concerning protection of former Presidents and their spouses by limiting the protection to ten years following the date the President leaves office.	1994
114 Stat. 2716	Congress authorizes USSS to plan, coordinate, and implement security at National Special Security Events, and established the National Threat Assessment Center within the Service.	2000
115 Stat. 277	Congress authorizes USSS to establish electronic crimes taskforces.	2001
116 Stat. 2224	Congress transfers USSS to DHS as a “distinct entity.”	2002

End notes

[1] The Homeland Security Act of 2002 (P.L. 107-296) transferred USSS to the newly created DHS. All of the Service's functions were transferred and it was to remain a "distinct" entity within DHS. Since being transferred to DHS in 2003, the USSS has continued to execute its investigative and protection missions.

[2] USSS would have been involved in President Obama's inauguration even if it had not been an NSSE because the Service is responsible for protecting the President.

[3] Of the 43 statutes referenced in this chapter, 26 were directly related to USSS's protection mission.

[4] U.S. Congress, House Committee on Appropriations' Subcommittee on Homeland Security, *Fiscal Year 2009 Budget for Secret Service's Candidate Protection*, 110th Cong., 2nd sess., April 3, 2008.

[5] U.S. Congress, House Committee on Homeland Security, *The U.S. Secret Service and Presidential Protection: An Examination of a System Failure*, 111th Cong., 1st sess., December 2, 2009.

[6] 116 Stat. 2224.

[7] U.S. Department of Homeland Security, U.S. Secret Service, "United States Secret Service: Investigative Mission," available at http://www.secretservice.gov/investigations.shtml.

[8] U.S. Department of Homeland Security, U.S. Secret Service, "United States Secret Service: Secret Service History," available at http://www.secretservice.gov/history.shtml.

[9] Financial crimes include identity theft, counterfeit and fraudulent identification, electronic access fraud, computer fraud, forgery, money laundering, electronic benefits transfer fraud, asset forfeiture, and advance fee. For a detailed definition of each of these crimes, see the U.S. Secret Service's website on "Criminal Investigations," available at http://www.secretservice.gov/criminal.shtml.

[10] U.S. Department of Homeland Security, U.S. Secret Service, "United States Secret Service: Forensic Services," website available at http://www.secretservice.gov/forensics.shtml.

[11] U.S. Department of Homeland Security, U.S. Secret Service, "United States Secret Service: Investigative Support," website available at *http://www.secretservice. gov/ in*vestigative_support.shtml.

[12] 108 Stat. 2043.

[13] 91 Stat. 3 authorized USSS to continue to protect specific federal officials who had received protection during the term of their employment; this was repealed in 1984 (98 Stat. 3110).

[14] This protection can not be declined.

[15] From this bullet forward, all of these individuals can decline protection.

[16] Former Presidents and spouses may receive protection for their lifetime, unless they serve in office after January 1, 1997 or decline the protection. If they serve after January 1, 1997, they are authorized to receive protection for 10 years after the date of leaving office and may decline the protection at any time.

[17] "Major" presidential and vice presidential candidates are determined by the DHS Secretary after consulting with an advisory committee. The advisory committee consists of the Speaker and minority leader of the House of Representatives, Senate majority and minority leaders, and one other member chosen by the committee.

[18] P.L. 110-326. This protection of former Vice Presidents and their families is for a period of not more than six months after the date the Vice President leaves office.

[19] Some of the issues addressed during an advanced survey include the assessment of manpower and equipment needs, and the location of hospitals. See USSS website on "Protection," available at http://www.secretservice.gov/ protection_works.shtml.

[20] U.S. Department of Homeland Security, U.S. Secret Service, "United States Secret Service: How Protection Works," website available at *http://www.secretservice. gov/ p*rotection _works.shtml.

[21] 18 U.S.C. 3056(e)-(f).
[22] Of the 43 statutes referenced in this chapter, 26 of them affect the service's protection mission.
[23] 2 Stat. 404.
[24] 12 Stat. 102.
[25] 12 Stat. 665.
[26] The U.S. National Archives & Records Administration, "Records of the U.S. Secret Service," website available at http://www.archives.gov/research/guide-fed-records/groups/087.html.
[27] Philip H. Melanson, and Peter F. Stevens, *The Secret Service: The Hidden History of an Enigmatic Agency*, New York, 2002, Carroll & Graf Publishers, p. 4.
[28] The U.S. National Archives & Records Administration, "Records of the U.S. Secret Service," website available at http://www.archives.gov/research/guide-fed-records/groups/087.html.
[29] Philip H. Melanson, and Peter F. Stevens, *The Secret Service: The Hidden History of an Enigmatic Agency*, p. 3.
[30] The U.S. National Archives & Records Administration, "Records of the U.S. Secret Service," website available at http://www.archives.gov/research/guide-fed-records/groups/087.html.
[31] Ibid. The Office of Solicitor of the Treasury was transferred to the Department of Justice in 1870 (16 Stat. 162), but continued to administer the SSD until 1879 even though the SSD remained within the Treasury Department.
[32] 22 Stat. 230.
[33] The protection mission, however, did not appear in statute until 1906.
[34] U.S. Department of Homeland Security, U.S. Secret Service, "United States Secret Service: Secret Service History," website available at http://www.secretservice.gov/history.shtml.
[35] 44 Stat. 918, and 48 Stat. 178.
[36] 62 Stat. 818.
[37] 76 Stat. 809 authorizes reimbursement to USSS for funds expended in purchasing counterfeit currency.
[38] 98 Stat. 2192. U.S. Department of Homeland Security, U.S. Secret Service, "United States Secret Service: Secret Service History," website available at *http://www.secretser* vice.gov/history.shtml.
[39] U.S. Department of Homeland Security, U.S. Secret Service, "United States Secret Service: Secret Service History," website available at http://www.secretservice.gov/history.shtml.
[40] 104 Stat. 1427.
[41] P.L. 107-56.
[42] 115 Stat. 277.
[43] U.S. Department of Homeland Security, U.S. Secret Service, "United States Secret Service: Secret Service History," website available at http://www.secretservice.gov/history.shtml, and Frederick Kaiser, "Origins of Secret Service Protection of the President: Personal, Interagency, and Institutional Conflict," *Presidential Studies Quarterly*, 1988, vol. XVIII, num. 1, p. 102. These early protective activities violated the strictures in the Service's appropriations that limited it to counterfeiting investigations.
[44] Frederick Kaiser, "Origins of Secret Service Protection of the President: Personal, Interagency, and Institutional Conflict," *Presidential Studies Quarterly*, 1988, vol. XVIII, no. 1, p. 112.
[45] Ibid.
[46] U.S. Department of Homeland Security, U.S. Secret Service, "United States Secret Service: Secret Service History," website available at http://www.secretservice.gov/history.shtml. For further information on presidential assassinations, see CRS Report RS20821, *Direct Assaults Against Presidents, Presidents-Elect, and Candidates*, by Frederick M. Kaiser.
[47] 34 Stat. 708.
[48] U.S. Department of Homeland Security, U.S. Secret Service, "United States Secret Service: Secret Service History," website available at http://www.secretservice.gov/history.shtml. According to the USSS, millions of acres were returned to the federal government as a result of the Service's investigations. In this case, Service agents were temporarily assigned

to the Departments of Justice and Interior to conduct the investigations, as neither department had a permanent investigation force.

[49] U.S. Department of Homeland Security, U.S. Secret Service, "United States Secret Service: Secret Service History," website available at http://www.secretservice.gov/history.shtml.

[50] Ibid.

[51] 38 Stat. 23. Congress continued to authorize this protection annually until 1951, when it permanently authorized USSS's protective mission in statute (65 Stat. 122).

[52] 39 Stat. 919.

[53] 40 Stat. 120.

[54] 42 Stat. 841.

[55] 46 Stat. 328.

[56] 57 Stat. 259-260.

[57] 65 Stat. 122.

[58] 67 Stat. 68. The U.S. National Archives & Records Administration, "Records of the U.S. Secret Service," website available at http://www.archives.gov/research/guide-fed-records/groups/.087.html.

[59] From 1951 to 1962, the Vice President was protected by USSS if "he so desired."

[60] 76 Stat. 956.

[61] 77 Stat. 348.

[62] 79 Stat. 791.

[63] 79 Stat. 890.

[64] 79 Stat. 791.

[65] 81 Stat. 466.

[66] 82 Stat. 1198.

[67] 82 Stat. 170. Presidential and vice presidential candidates could decline protection.

[68] Ibid.

[69] 84 Stat. 74-75. USSS states, on their website, that it assumed the protection of foreign diplomatic missions outside of the metropolitan DC area in 1975. This document is available at http://www.secretservice.gov/history.shtml.

[70] 91 Stat. 1371.

[71] 84 Stat. 1941. One of the "distinguished foreign visitors" to receive USSS protection was Pope Benedict in April 2008.

[72] Ibid.

[73] 84 Stat. 1892.

[74] 88 Stat. 1765.

[75] 90 Stat. 2475. This activity arose in the aftermath of concerns that the security arrangements at multiple private residences were excessive and not adequately justified. See House Committee on Government Operations, Expenditures of Federal Funds in Support of Presidential Properties, H.Rept. 93-1052 (GPO, 1974), pp. 1-6.

[76] 90 Stat. 1239.

[77] 91 Stat. 3. The individual had to be an official who had been receiving USSS protection before 1977, and the President had to determine the former official still needed protection. This provision was repealed in 1984. 98 Stat. 3110.

[78] 94 Stat. 2740.

[79] 96 Stat. 1451.

[80] 98 Stat. 3110.

[81] 108 Stat. 2412-2413. "The protection of a former President will end ten years from the date a former President leaves office, if the President served in office after January 1, 1997. Protection of the spouse of a former President will terminate in the event of remarriage or divorce from a former President. If the President dies in office or within one year of office, the spouse will receive protection for one year from the time of death. Provided, that the Department of Homeland Security Secretary has the authority to direct USSS to provide

temporary protection for any of these individuals at anytime the Secretary or designee determines that conditions or information warrant such protection." 18 U.S.C. §3056(a)(3).

[82] U.S. Department of Homeland Security, U.S. Secret Service, "United States Secret Service: Secret Service History," website available at http://www.secretservice.gov/history.shtml.

[83] President Richard M. Nixon declined USSS protection after leaving office.

[84] Additionally, in 1995 a portion of Pennsylvania Avenue was closed off to vehicular traffic due to the bombing of the James Murrah Building in Oklahoma City, Oklahoma.

[85] Presidential Decision Directive 62 is classified. The White House issued a fact sheet abstract about it, and the Federation of American Scientists has posted an "unclassified abstract" said to be "derived from" PDD 62, available at http://www.fas.org/irp/offdocs/pdd-62.htm.

[86] 114 Stat. 2716.

[87] Ibid.

[88] P.L. 110-329, Title II and P.L. 111-8, Div. J.

[89] P.L. 110-161, Div. E, Title V, Sec. 516.

[90] Philip H. Melanson, and Peter F. Stevens, *The Secret Service: The Hidden History of an Enigmatic Agency*, p. 333.

[91] Philip H. Melanson, and Peter F. Stevens, *The Secret Service: The Hidden History of an Enigmatic Agency*, p. 335.

[92] U.S. Congress, House Committee on Appropriation's Subcommittee on Homeland Security, *Fiscal Year 2009 Budget for Secret Service's Candidate Protection*, hearing, 110th Cong., 2nd sess., April 3, 2008, p. 2.

[93] Ibid., p. 3.

[94] Ibid., p. 4.

[95] Ibid., p. 8. At the hearing USSS Director Sullivan stated that it costs approximately $44,000 a day to protect a presidential candidate.

[96] The homeland security strategy is available at http://www.whitehouse. gov/infocus/ homeland/ nshs/NSHS.pdf.

[97] U.S. Department of Treasury, "Duties and Functions Mission," available at *http://www.* treas.gov/ education/duties/.

[98] 31 U.S.C. 310(C).

[99] 31 U.S.C. 311(a)(2).

[100] 31 U.S.C. 313(a)(4).

[101] U.S. Department of Homeland Security, "Strategic Plan -Securing Our Homeland," available at http://www.dhs.gov/ xabout/strategicplan/index.shtm.

[102] 6 U.S.C. 111(b)(1)(A).

[103] 6 U.S.C. 111(b)(1)(B).

[104] Office of the President, National Homeland Security Council, *National Strategy for Homeland Security*, p. 1, available at http://www.whitehouse.gov/infocus/homeland/nshs/NSHS.pdf.

[105] For a detailed list of assassination attempts, see CRS Report RS20821, *Direct Assaults Against Presidents, Presidents-Elect, and Candidates*, by Frederick M. Kaiser.

[106] U.S. Department of Homeland Security, U.S. Secret Service, "United States Secret Service: National Threat Assessment Center," available at http://www.secretservice. gov/ntac.

[107] Ibid.

[108] Office of the President, National Homeland Security Council, *National Strategy for Homeland Security*, p. 27.

[109] U.S. Department of Homeland Security, "Office of Infrastructure Protection," available at http://www.dhs.gov/ xabout/structure/gc_1185203138955.shtm.

[110] Federal Bureau of Investigation, "About Us-Quick Facts," available at *http://www* .fbi.gov/quickfacts.htm.

[111] For detailed information on assaults against Presidents, Presidents-Elect, and candidates (those with and without Security Service protection), see CRS Report RS20821, *Direct Assaults Against Presidents, Presidents-Elect, and Candidates*, by Frederick M. Kaiser.

[112] U.S. Congress, House Committee on Homeland Security, *The U.S. Secret Service and Presidential Protection: An Examination of a System Failure*, 111th Cong., 1st sess., December 2, 2009.

[113] Ibid.

[114] 39 Stat. 919.

In: Financial Crimes: Fraud, Theft…
Editors: Jonathan G. McDougal
ISBN: 978-1-61122-479-5

Chapter 2

CHECK CASHERS AND BANKER'S DISCONTINUANCE OF SERVICES

Pauline Smale and Walter W. Eubanks

SUMMARY

A check cashing enterprise is a fee-based business that will cash a customer's check without requiring an account relationship. The U.S. check cashing industry underwent a significant expansion in the 1990s. Customers are attracted by the immediate access to funds, availability of service without a bank account, and convenience of extended hours of operation. In general, the industry is viewed as a provider of valuable financial services to an under served market segment.

Check cashers are dependent on access to bank services to operate. Banks provide depository accounts, check collection and clearing operations, funds transfer, and access to lines of credit for liquidity purposes. Banks and check cashers are both subject to Bank Secrecy Act (BSA)[1] regulations. The BSA is an anti-money laundering and anti-terrorism financing statute. Federal regulators have cautioned banks that nonbank money service businesses (an umbrella term that includes check cashing enterprises) can present heightened money laundering risks. Consequently, some banks have discontinued their business relations with check cashers. The discontinuance of services to check cashers brought about complaints to regulators and increased lobbying of

Congress. Bank regulators have issued guidance to clarify BSA compliance expectations. Congress held hearings on the concerns of banks and check cashers.

INTRODUCTION

Check cashers are nonbank businesses that cash checks for a fee. Check cashing businesses may offer additional fee-based products and services including money orders, processing utility bill payments, pre-paid phone cards, and funds transfers. These enterprises often operate in neighborhoods not well served by banks. Check cashers provide access to financial services for individuals without accounts at conventional banks. To provide these services, a check cashing enterprise establishes a business relationship with a bank to clear checks, transfer funds, and open lines of credit for liquidity purposes.

The Bank Secrecy Act regulations define check cashers as money services businesses (MSBs). Both banks and nonbank MSBs must have written anti-money laundering programs, file currency transaction reports (CRTs) and supicious activity reports (SARs), and maintain certain records. MSBs, including check cashers, must register with the Financial Crimes Enforcement Network (FinCEN), a bureau of the U.S. Treasury. Banks providing services to check cashers are expected to have systems to manage the risks associated with these accounts.

The following developments created difficulties to obtaining and maintaining access to banking services.

- The Office of the Comptroller of Currency (OCC) a federal bank regulatory agency included check cashers and other MSBs in a list of inherently high-risk businesses in its Bank Secrecy Act/ Anti-Money Laundering Manual.
- The OCC has also stated that the risk profiles of individual businesses can vary widely based on the variety and range of financial services offered.
- FinCEN strengthened BSA enforcement after the enactment of the USA PATRIOT Act[2] and with the increased focus on terrorism financing after 9/11.

- Banker's compliance costs were affected by the risks associated with a check cashing business.
- Substantial fines were levied by bank regulators on banking institutions for BSA non-compliance.

The potential price of doing business proved to be prohibitive for a number of banks, resulting in discontinuance of services to check cashers.

In April 2005, bank regulators issued interagency guidance[3] in response to concerns over the loss of access to banking services by check cashers and other MSBs. Concern is twofold: (1) widespread termination of account relationships could result in the loss of access to financial services and products by the significant market segment currently served by check cashers and (2) if these businesses are consequently forced "underground" the potential loss of transparency could damage ongoing efforts to safeguard the U.S. financial system. The guidance addressed both the ability of check cashers and other MSBs to obtain services and the caution to be maintained by banks dealing with these businesses. The goal was to clarify the regulatory expectations for banking institutions providing services to domestic businesses. It is generally acknowledged that the trend of individual banks terminating account relationships with check cashers has continued. On June 21, 2006, the Subcommittee on Financial Institutions and Consumer Credit of the House Financial Services Committee held an oversight hearing to assess the impact of the BSA obligations on check cashers and other MSBs.

Background

The Industry. The nonbank check cashing industry can trace its origins back to the 1930's when employers began paying workers by check as opposed to cash. Workers without traditional bank accounts used check cashers, where an account relationship is not required, to convert those paychecks into cash for a fee. Today's check cashing enterprise may offer additional fee-based products and services including money orders, processing utility bill payments, pre-paid phone cards and funds transfers. Money transfers may include foreign worker remittances (money sent back to the workers' home countries). Some also offer credit products such as payday loans, where customers are given cash for a postdated personal check for the amount of cash requested plus the check casher's fee. Check cashing services can be offered as an ancillary component of a business, such as a liquor stores that cashes payroll checks. Items cashed are primarily payroll checks, government checks, personal checks, cashier's checks, money orders, and traveler's checks. The typical value of a cashed item ranges from $300 to $600.[4] Most fees range from 1% to 12% of the check's value.[5] The main financial risk for the check casher is a returned check unpaid by the bank on which it was drawn. Fees vary by type of check. For example, the fee for a personal check is usually greater than for a government check. Many states require a license for check cashing enterprises and/or regulate their fee structures. Some states have additional restrictions for pay day lending.[6]

The check cashing industry has experienced a period of significant growth since the early 1990's. One estimate for 1990 indicated that the check cashing industry comprised approximately 4,250 businesses that cashed 128 million checks with a total face value of $38 billion.[7] In 2002, an estimated 11,000 check cashing enterprises cashed approximately 180 million checks with a total face value of $55 billion.[8] Customers are drawn to check cashers for a variety of reasons. Check cashers typically offer convenient hours of service that extend beyond the normal hours of operation found at mainstream banking institutions. The barriers involved with opening an account at a bank such as minimum account balances, specific identification requirements, and credit checks are not encountered. In addition, the check holder is not subject to the variety of fees and services charges typically associated with a bank account. A customer's funds are immediately available while banks may impose check clearing holds.

Customers of check cashing businesses tend to be low and moderate income consumers. The so called "unbanked" consumers rely on alternative financial services offered by nonbanks. There are a significant number of unbanked families in the United States; they do not hold a checking or savings account at a federally insured financial institution. Studies vary, but it is generally estimated that about 10 million U.S. households do not own a bank account.[9] The costs associated with maintaining accounts, dislike of banking institutions, and the convenience offered by alternative nonbank service providers are among the more frequently given reasons for their popularity. Conversely, it is estimated that 58% of the check cashing industry's clientele are bank account holders.[10]

Bank Secrecy Act. In 1970, the Bank Secrecy Act was enacted to create a federal anti-money laundering program. In 2001, Title 111 of the USA PATRIOT ACT[11] amended the BSA with provisions to strengthen the existing program and to counter terrorist financing. The Financial Crimes Enforcement Network, a bureau of the U.S. Treasury Department, administers and issues regulations pursuant to the BSA. Check cashing enterprises that meet the definition of a money service business are required to register with FinCEN.[12] Banks providing services to check cashers are expected to have in place systems to manage the risks associated with these accounts.

BSA reporting and record keeping requirements apply to both banks and MSBs. Both must establish anti-money laundering programs commensurate with the risks posed by their size, location and financial activities. Both are required to file currency transaction reports (CTRs) for cash transactions over $10,000 and to maintain a log on the sale of financial products such as money orders or travelers checks valued from $3,000 to $10,000. Information must also be maintained on funds transfer of $3,000 or more. Finally, MSBs are required to file suspicious activity reports (SARs).[13] FinCEN has delegated the authority to examine check cashers for BSA compliance to the Internal Revenue Service (IRS).[14]

2005 Interagency Guidance. The intent of the interagency guidelines was to clarify the supervisory expectations of banks to remain in compliance with the requirements of the BSA while providing services to check cashers and other MSBs. The guidance was issued to assist banks in developing appropriate BSA risk assessments. Another goal was to help ensure check cashers and other MSBs have reasonable access to banking services. Concurrent with the 2005 guidance, an advisory was issued addressing the BSA obligations of check cashers and outlining the documentation an MSB may be expected to provide when establishing an account relationship at a bank. The advisory was issued as part of an ongoing campaign to inform MSBs about their BSA requirements. FinCEN has recognized that outreach to the MSB industry is essential; they found that many of the businesses, especially the smaller operations, are unfamiliar or unaware of their obligations.

The 2005 interagency guidance directed banks opening and maintaining accounts for MSBs to apply the requirements of the BSA on a risk-assessed basis. Five minimum due diligence expectations are presented: (1) apply the bank's Customer Identification Program, (2) confirm FinCEN registration, (3) confirm compliance with state or local licensing requirements, (4) confirm agent status (many MSBs operate through a system of agents), and (5) conduct a basic Bank Secrecy Act/Anti-Money Laundering risk assessment to determine the level of risk associated with the potential account and whether further due diligence is necessary. The guidance outlines further due diligence criteria, beyond the minimum expectations, that may be called for by the risk profile of the individual money service business.[15]

Banks' relationship with Check Cashers. Check cashers require specific banking services to operate. These financial services include depository accounts, check collection and clearing operations, funds transfer, and access to lines of credit for liquidity purposes. Banks generate fee income for financial services provided. An individual banking institution's experience with check cashers is often dependent on the proximity between the two. Some banks specialize in servicing check cashers. Consequently, the decision of an individual bank to discontinue services to check cashers could have a significant impact. For example, according to the Financial Services Center of America (FISCA), in New York 12 banks currently provide services to check cashers but 87% of the 640 licensed check cashers do business with only two of these banks.[16]

BSA compliance requirements and supervisory expectations are viewed as burdensome and have caused banks to re-evaluate the costs and benefits of opening and maintaining accounts for check cashers. Banking representatives testifying at the June 2006 oversight hearing stated that the level of BSA risk assessment and monitoring required of them by the regulatory agencies remains burdensome and costly despite the 2005 guidance. Of particular concern is determining the delineation between low and high risk profiles and the corresponding *due diligence* expectations. In addition, bankers suggested that regulators should not expect a bank's monitoring activity to extend beyond the check cashing business to the activity of the check casher's customers. They argue FinCEN should further clarify that banks are not expected to be de facto regulators of check cashers by instituting a system that more clearly defines the responsibility for oversight of the BSA obligations of check cashers and other MSBs.

Policy Issues

In March 2006, a FinCEN news release[17] acknowledged the ongoing concerns of both the banking industry and money service businesses relating to BSA regulations despite the previous steps taken (including the April 2005 guidance) to address the issues. The difficulties involve how to minimize the resources and costs borne by financial institutions while ensuring the effective administration of the anti-terrorism financing and anti-money laundering programs. The news release announced an Advanced Notice of Proposed Rulemaking seeking input on what additional guidance or regulatory action would be appropriate to address the ongoing concerns about check casher's and other MSB's access to banking services. The news release emphasized the important role of MSBs and the negative effect on the health and safety of the U.S. financial system if these businesses are driven underground. Comments received by FinCEN are under review and potential next steps are being considered.

On June 21, 2006, the Subcommittee on Financial Institutions and Consumer Credit of the House Committee on Financial Services held an oversight hearing on the Bank Secrecy Act's impact on money services businesses. There was general agreement that banks were re-evaluating their businesses strategies in light of BSA *due diligence* costs. There were reports of individual institutions concluding that opening and maintaining accounts for MSBs did not make economic sense. Regulatory and supervisory adjustments were discussed as a means of easing the burden on banks. Stronger state MSB regulatory oversight was encouraged. Joint industry/government training on BSA obligations for banks, bank examiners, and MSBs was suggested. In addition, FiSCA (the trade association, representing 6,000 check cashing operations and nonbank financial service centers), suggested the need for legislation that would remove state regulated check cashers from "high risk" categories. In its view, legislation could also limit administrative enforcement actions against banks that service check cashers in good faith.

End Notes

[1] P.L. 91-508.

[2] P.L. 107-56.

[3] Financial Crimes Enforcement Network, "Interagency Interpretive Guidance on Providing Banking Services to Money Services Businesses Operating in the United States," joint press release, Apr. 26, 2005, at [http://www.fincen.gov/nr04262005.pdf].

[4] Catherine Stahlmann, "Check Cashers and Money Transmitters Serious Risks or Just Misunderstood?," Federal Reserve Bank of Atlanta, May 2003, p. 3.

[5] Howard Karger, *Shortchanged; Life and Debt in the Fringe Economy* (San Francisco: Berrett-Koehler, 2005), p.89.

[6] Information on state laws can be found on the National Conference of State Legislatures website, [http://www.ncl.org].

[7] John P. Caskey, *Fringe Banking: Check-Cashing Outlets, Pawnshops, and the Poor* (New York: Russell Sage Foundation), p. 65.

[8] Howard Karger, *Shortchanged; Life and Debt in the Fringe Economy*, San Francisco: Berrett-Koehler, 2005), p. 6.

[9] Michael S. Barr, "Banking the Poor," a working paper prepared for the Brookings Institution Center on Urban and Metropolitan Policy, July 2003, p.8.

[10] Catherine Stahlmann, "Check Cashers and Money Transmitters Serious Risks or Just Misunderstood?", Federal Reserve Bank of Atlanta, May 2003. p. 2.

[11] P.L. 107-56. For more detailed information on this act and pre-existing law, see CRS Report RL31208, *International Money Laundering Abatement and Anti-Terrorist Financing Act of 2001,Title 111 of P.L.107-56*, by M. Maureen Murphy.

[12] Nonbank MSBs are defined as a business offering one or more of the following services: money orders, traveler's checks, check cashing, currency dealing or exchange, and stored value. In addition, registration with FinCEN is required if the business conducts more than $1,000 in money services business activity with the same person in one day or provides money transfer services in any amount.

[13] For detailed information on BSA requirements for MSBs, see *Money Laundering Prevention: A Money Services Business Guide*, found at the MSB website, at [http://www.msb.gov].

[14] For more information on the IRS compliance monitoring, see CRS Report RS22003, *Enforcement of Bank Secrecy Act Requirements: Money Services Businesses*, by Nathan Brooks.

[15] The full text of the interpretive guidance can be found on FinCEN's website at [http://www.fincen.gov/nr04262005.pdf].

[16] Testimony of Gerald Goldman, General Counsel, Financial Services Center of America, before the U.S. Congress, House Committee, Subcommitee of Financial Institution and Consumer Credit, *Bank Secrecy Act's Impact on Money Services Businesses*, June 26, 2006, p. 2 [http://financialservices.house.gov/media/pdf/062106gg.pdf].

[17] The full text of the news release and the text of the Advanced Notice of Proposed Rulemaking from the March 10, 2006 Federal Register, can be found on FinCEN's website [http://www.fincen.gov/msb_anpr.pdf].

In: Financial Crimes: Fraud, Theft… ISBN: 978-1-61122-479-5
Editors: Jonathan G. McDougal

Chapter 3

Credit Card Accountability Responsibility and Disclosure Act of 2009 (H.R. 627)

Congressional Reference Service

5/22/2009--Public Law. (This measure has not been amended since it was passed by the Senate on May 19, 2009. The summary of that version is repeated here.) Credit Card Accountability Responsibility and Disclosure Act of 2009 or the Credit CARD Act of 2009 -

Section 2

Authorizes the Board of Governors of the Federal Reserve System (Federal Reserve Board) to issue rules and publish model forms to implement this Act.

Section 3

Makes this Act effective nine months after its enactment.

TITLE I - CONSUMER PROTECTION

Section 101

Amends the Truth in Lending Act (TILA), with respect to credit card accounts under an open end consumer credit plan, to require a creditor to provide written notice not later than 45 days prior to the effective date of: (1) any increase in an annual percentage rate (APR); and (2) any significant change, as determined by rule of the Federal Reserve Board, in the terms of the cardholder agreement (including an increase in fees or finance charges). Prohibits a creditor from increasing any annual percentage rate (APR) of interest, fee, or finance charge applicable to the existing balance on an open end consumer credit card account unless specified conditions are met. Allows a creditor to increase an APR, fee, or finance charge only if the increase is due solely to: (1) expiration of a specified time period (e.g., promotional period) disclosed clearly and conspicuously to the consumer before commencement of the time period; (2) a change in index not under the creditor's control; (3) payment not received during the 30-day grace period after the due date; or (4) completion of a workout or temporary hardship arrangement, or the consumer's failure to comply with such an arrangement. Prohibits any APR increase relating to such an arrangement from exceeding the APR applicable to the particular category of transactions on the day before the effective date of the arrangement. Prohibits a creditor from changing the terms governing repayment of an outstanding balance; but permits the creditor to provide the obligor with specified repayment methods. Requires a creditor that increases the APR based upon factors including the obligor's credit risk, market conditions, or other factors to: (1) consider changes in such factors in subsequently determining whether to reduce the APR for such obligor; and (2) reduce the APR when a review indicates a reduction. Declares that no increase in any APR, fee, or finance charge, with certain exceptions, shall be effective before the end of the one-year period beginning on the date on which the account is opened. States that, in the case of a promotional rate, no written notice of an increase in the APR shall be effective before the end of a six-month period beginning from the date the promotional rate takes effect.

Section 102

Prohibits imposition of a finance charge, with certain exceptions, upon a credit card account balance that is based on balances for days in billing cycles preceding the most recent billing cycle (double billing cycle) as a result of the loss of any grace period. Prohibits penalties for on-time payments. Prohibits the charge of an over-the-limit fee unless the consumer expressly permits the creditor to complete the relevant transaction (opt-in). Allows imposition of an over-the-limit fee only once during a billing cycle. Prohibits its imposition more than once in two subsequent billing cycles with respect to such excess credit, unless the consumer: (1) has obtained an additional extension of credit in excess of the credit limit during any such subsequent cycle; or (2) reduces the outstanding balance below the credit limit as of the end of such billing cycle. Prohibits a creditor from imposing a separate fee related to the method of payment (by mail, electronic transfer, telephone authorization, or other means), unless the payment involves an expedited service by the creditor's service representative. Requires any penalty fee or charge to be reasonable and proportional to the omission or violation involved. Directs the Federal Reserve Board to establish standards for assessing whether the amount of any penalty fee or charge is reasonable and proportional to the omission or violation to which the fee or charge relates.

Section 103

Limits the use of the term "fixed," in conjunction with an APR or applicable interest rate, to a rate that will not change or vary for any reason over the period specified clearly and conspicuously in the terms of the account.

Section 104

Revises requirements governing crediting of payments. Requires a card issuer, upon receipt of payment, to apply amounts in excess of the minimum payment amount first to the balance bearing the highest rate of interest, and then to each successive balance bearing the next highest rate of interest, until the payment is exhausted. Requires a creditor to allocate the entire amount paid in excess of the minimum payment to a balance on which interest is deferred during the last two billing cycles immediately preceding the expiration of the period during which interest is deferred. Prohibits a card issuer from imposing any late fee or finance charge for a late payment if: (1) the issuer makes a material change in the mailing address, office, or procedures for handling cardholder payments; and (2) such change causes a material delay in the crediting of payment made during the 60-day period following the date on which such change took effect.

Section 105

Prescribes a standard for the initial issuance of subprime or "fee harvester" cards (accounts requiring first-year fee payments in excess of 25% of the total amount of credit authorized). Prohibits payment of any fee from the credit made available by the card (other than any late fee, over-the-limit fee, or any fee for a payment returned for insufficient funds).

Section 106

Requires the payment due date to be the same day each month, or the next business day if such date falls on a weekend or holiday. Revises requirements for the timing of payments and the grace period. Requires each periodic statement of payment due to be mailed no later than 21 days before the payment due date.

Section 107

Revises civil penalties for creditor noncompliance with TILA. Includes in such penalties twice the amount of any finance charge in connection with a transaction, between $500 and $5,000 (or a higher amount in the case of an established pattern or practice of noncompliance), in the case of an individual action relating to an open end consumer credit plan that is not secured by real property or a dwelling.

Section 109

Requires a card issuer to consider the ability of the consumer to make required payments as a prerequisite to opening any consumer credit card account, or increasing any credit limit.

TITLE II - ENHANCED CONSUMER DISCLOSURES

Section 201

Revises and expands requirements for mandatory minimum payment disclosures a creditor must furnish. Directs the Federal Reserve Board to issue guidelines, by rule, for the establishment and maintenance by creditors of a toll-free telephone number for purposes of providing information about accessing credit counseling and debt management services.

Section 202

Revises requirements relating to late payment deadlines. Requires specified disclosures relating to increases in interest rates for late payments. States that the date on which the obligor makes a payment at the local branch of a creditor financial institution shall be considered to be the date on which the payment is made for purposes of determining whether a late fee or charge may be imposed due to the failure of the obligor to make payment on or before the due date for such payment.

Section 203

Requires a card issuer that has changed or amended any term of the account since the last renewal that has not been previously disclosed to make such a disclosure to the consumer by a certain deadline.

Section 204

Requires creditors to post on an Internet site the written agreement between the creditor and the consumer for each open-end consumer credit plan.

Section 205

Amends the Fair Credit Reporting Act to require any advertisement for a free credit report to disclose prominently that free credit reports are available under federal law at AnnualCreditReport.com (or other authorized source).

TITLE III - PROTECTION OF YOUNG CONSUMERS

Section 301

Amends TILA to prohibit extensions of credit to consumers under age 21, unless the consumer has submitted a written application that meets specified requirements. Requires any such application to be signed by a cosigner, including the parent, legal guardian, spouse, or any other individual who has attained the age of 21 having a means to repay debts incurred by the consumer in connection with the account.

Section 302

Amends the Fair Credit Reporting Act to permit a consumer reporting agency to furnish a consumer report regarding credit or insurance transactions that are not initiated by the consumer only if the report does not contain a date of birth that shows that the consumer has not attained the age of 21, or, if the date of birth on the consumer report shows that the consumer has not attained the age of 21, the consumer consents to the furnishing of such report.

Section 303

Amends TILA to require approval by the jointly liable party to increase credit lines for accounts for which a parent, legal guardian, spouse of the consumer, or any other individual is jointly liable.

Section 304

Requires an institution of higher education to disclose publicly any agreement made with a card issuer or creditor for the purpose of marketing a credit card. Prohibits a card issuer or creditor from offering to a student at an institution of higher education any tangible item as inducement to participate in an open end consumer credit plan if such offer is made: (1) on or near the campus of the institution; or (2) at an event sponsored by or related to such institution. Expresses the sense of Congress that each institution of higher education should consider adopting the following policies relating to credit cards: (1) that any card issuer that markets a credit card on the campus notify the institution of the location at which such marketing will take place; (2) that the number of locations on the campus at which the marketing of credit cards takes place be limited; and (3) that credit card and debt education and counseling sessions be offered as a regular part of any orientation program for new students.

Section 305

Requires each creditor to submit an annual report to the Federal Reserve Board containing the terms and conditions of all business, marketing, and promotional agreements and college affinity card agreements with an institution of higher education, or with an affiliated or related alumni organization or foundation, with respect to any college student credit card issued to a college student at such institution. Directs to the Federal Reserve Board to report to Congress, and make available to the public, on the information concerning credit card agreements submitted to it by each institution of higher education, alumni organization, or foundation. Directs the Comptroller General to review and report to Congress about the mandatory reports submitted by creditors as well as their marketing practices to determine the impact that college affinity card agreements and college student card agreements have upon credit card debt.

Title IV - Gift Cards

Section 401

Amends the Electronic Fund Transfer Act to declare unlawful: (1) the imposition of a dormancy fee, an inactivity charge or fee, or a service fee with respect to a gift certificate, store gift card, or general-use prepaid card; and (2) the sale or issuance of a gift certificate, store gift card, or general-use prepaid card that is subject to an expiration date.

Title V - Miscellaneous Provisions

Section 501

Instructs the Comptroller General to study and report to Congress on use of credit by consumers, interchange fees, and their effects on consumers and merchants.

Section 502

Directs the Federal Reserve Board to review biennially and report to Congress on specified aspects of the consumer credit card market. Directs the federal banking agencies and the Federal Trade Commission (FTC) to report annually to the Federal Reserve Board, for inclusion in its annual report to Congress, on their regulatory activities regarding credit card issuer compliance with federal consumer protection statutes and regulations.

Section 503

Directs the Secretary of the Treasury to issue regulations implementing the Bank Secrecy Act regarding the sale, issuance, redemption, or international transport of stored value, including stored value cards.

Section 504

Amends TILA to direct the Federal Reserve Board to prescribe regulations to require creditors to establish procedures to ensure that any administrator of the estate of any deceased obligor can resolve outstanding credit balances of the estate in a timely manner.

Section 505

Directs the Federal Reserve Board to report to certain congressional committees on the extent to which creditors have reduced credit limits or raised interest rates applicable to credit card accounts based on specified factors, including the geographical location of a credit transaction, the identity of the merchant involved, the consumer's credit transactions, and the identity of a consumer's mortgage creditor.

Section 506

Directs the Federal Reserve Board to review and report to Congress on: (1) the use of credit cards by small businesses with not more than 50 employees; and (2) the credit card market for such businesses.

Section 507

Directs the Administrator of the Small Business Administration (SBA), in conjunction with the Secretary of Homeland Security, to establish the Small Business Information Security Task Force to: (1) address the information technology security needs of small business concerns; and (2) help them prevent the loss of credit card data. Requires the task force to make recommendations to the SBA Administrator about establishment of an Internet website to receive and dispense information and resources with respect to: (1) the information technology security needs of small business concerns; and (2) the programs and services provided by the federal government, state governments, and nongovernment organizations (NGOs) that serve those needs. Requires the task force to make recommendations also relating to developing additional education materials and programs with respect to information technology security needs. Authorizes appropriations for FY2020-FY2013.

Section 508

Directs the FTC to study and report to Congress on the cost-effectiveness of making technology available at an automated teller machines (ATM) that enables a consumer under duress to alert a local law enforcement agency electronically that an incident is taking place at the ATM.

Section 509

Directs the Comptroller General to study and report to Congress on the terms, conditions, marketing, and value to consumers of products marketed in conjunction with credit card offers.

Section 510

Directs the Secretary of Education and the Director of the Office of Financial Education of the Department of the Treasury to coordinate with the President's Advisory Council on Financial Literacy to report to Congress on: (1) their evaluation and compilation of a comprehensive summary of existing federal financial and economic literacy education programs; and (2) development of a strategic plan to improve and expand financial and economic literacy education.

Section 511

Amends the Omnibus Appropriations Act, 2009 to direct the FTC to initiate a rulemaking on unfair or deceptive acts or practices with respect to mortgage loans, loan modification, and foreclosure rescue services. Denies the FTC authority to promulgate a rule regarding an entity that is not subject to its enforcement powers. Authorizes a state, as parens patriae, to bring a civil action on behalf of its residents if the state attorney general believes that an interest of state residents is threatened or adversely affected by action of any person subject to an FTC-prescribed rule in a practice that violates such rule.

Section 512

Prohibits the Secretary of the Interior from promulgating or enforcing any regulation that prohibits an individual from possessing a firearm, including an assembled or functional firearm, in any unit of the National Park System (NPS) or the National Wildlife Refuge System (NWRS) if: (1) the individual is not otherwise prohibited by law from possessing the firearm; and (2) the possession of the firearm complies with the law of the state in which the NPS or NWRS unit is located.

Section 513

Requires the Comptroller General to study and report to Congress on: (1) the relationship between fluency in the English language and financial literacy; and (2) any extent to which individuals whose native language is a language other than English are impeded in their conduct of their financial affairs.

In: Financial Crimes: Fraud, Theft…
Editors: Jonathan G. McDougal
ISBN: 978-1-61122-479-5

Chapter 4

WALL STREET REFORM AND CONSUMER PROTECTION ACT OF 2009*

Congressional Research Service

TITLE I - FINANCIAL STABILITY IMPROVEMENT ACT

Financial Stability Improvement Act of 2009 - (Sec. 1000A) Directs the Comptroller General to audit and report to Congress within two years after enactment of this Act on all actions taken by the Board of Governors of the Federal Reserve System (Federal Reserve Board) and the federal reserve banks during the current economic crisis.

Subtitle A - The Financial Services Oversight Council

Section 1001

Establishes the Financial Services Oversight Council, consisting of the heads of specified federal financial regulatory bodies and chaired by the Secretary of the Treasury. Requires the Council, among other things, to: (1) advise Congress on financial domestic and international regulatory developments, including insurance and accounting developments, and make

* Congressional Research Service Summary

recommendations to enhance the integrity, efficiency, competitiveness, and stability of the U.S. financial markets; (2) monitor the financial services marketplace to identify potential threats to the stability of the U.S. financial system; (3) subject financial companies and activities to stricter prudential standards; (4) recommend that a member Council agency adopt stricter prudential standards for the firms it regulates in order to mitigate systemic risk; and (5) resolve, upon request, a jurisdictional dispute between member Council agencies.

Section 1006

Requires the Council to report semiannually to designated congressional committees regarding: (1) significant financial and regulatory developments and their impact upon the stability of the financial system; and (2) strategies developed in response to potential threats to the stability of the U.S. financial system. Directs the Council to study the effects that regulations and standards of the Consumer Financial Protection Agency (CFPA), established under this Act, will have upon covered persons, including nondepository institutions. Requires the study to include an assessment of the appropriateness of using "APR" (Annual Percentage Rate) as a true measure of the value of all nonbank products.

Section 1008

Authorizes the Comptroller General to audit and report periodically to certain congressional committees on Council activities and financial transactions.

Subtitle B - Prudential Regulation of Companies and Activities for Financial Stability Purposes

Section 1100

Empowers the Federal Reserve Board to act as agent for the Council, and to act on its behalf.

Section 1101

Authorizes the Council and the Federal Reserve Board to receive, and to request the production of, any data or information from Council members in order to: (1) monitor the financial services marketplace to identify potential threats to the stability of the U.S. Financial system; (2) identify global trends and developments that could pose systemic risks to the stability of the U.S. economy or other economies; or (3) ascertain a primary financial regulatory agency's implementation of recommended prudential standards.

Section 1102

Authorizes the Council to make formal recommendations that a federal financial regulatory agency adopt stricter prudential standards for firms it regulates in order to mitigate systemic risk. Authorizes a federal financial regulatory agency to implement increased oversight in response to Council recommendations.

Section 1103

Directs the Council to subject a financial activity or practice to stricter prudential standards for financial stability purposes upon making specified determinations that: (1) material financial distress at the company could pose a threat to financial stability or the economy; or (2) the nature, scope, size, scale, concentration, and interconnectedness, or mix of the company's activities could pose a threat to financial stability or to the economy. Requires the Federal Reserve Board to report periodically to the Council whether a company subjected to stricter prudential standards should continue under such standards. Subjects the stricter prudential standards, upon company appeal, to judicial review. Directs the Board to require each financial holding company subject to stricter standards to maintain a debt to equity ratio of no more than 15 to 1 (leverage limitation).

Section 1104

Directs the Federal Reserve Board, as agent of the Council, to impose specified stricter prudential standards on a financial holding company on which the Council has already imposed stricter prudential standards. Requires the computation of capital requirements for any financial holding company subject to stricter standards to take into account specified off balance sheet activities of the company. Prescribes circumstances for discretionary imposition of stricter prudential standards on functionally regulated subsidiaries or subsidiary depository institutions of a financial holding company subject to stricter standards. Requires the Board to prescribe standards that limit to 25% (or a lower percentage) of capital stock and surplus (concentration limits) of the financial holding company subject to stricter standards the risks posed by the credit exposure of such a company to any unaffiliated company. Exempts the federal home loan banks from such limitations. Authorizes the Board to limit the amount of short-term debt that may be accumulated by any financial holding company subject to stricter standards, including off-balance sheet exposures. Requires the Board to: (1) take specified prompt corrective action to resolve the problems of financial holding companies subject to stricter standards; and (2) specify for each relevant capital measure the levels at which a financial holding company subject to stricter standards is well capitalized, undercapitalized, and significantly undercapitalized. Restricts the asset growth of an under capitalized financial holding company that is subject to stricter standards. Requires such a company to obtain the Federal Reserve Board's written approval prior to: (1) paying a bonus to any senior executive officer; and (2) providing compensation to any senior executive officer at a rate exceeding that officer's average rate of compensation (excluding bonuses, stock options, and profit-sharing) during the 12 calendar months preceding the calendar month in which the financial holding company subject to stricter standards became undercapitalized. Grants the Federal Reserve Board enforcement authority over a foreign financial holding company subject to stricter standards if the Board believes that its condition, practice, or activity is not in compliance with this Act. Requires a financial holding company subject to stricter standards to submit a rapid resolution plan to address the results of stress tests that indicate significant or critical undercapitalization. Directs the Federal Deposit Insurance Corporation (FDIC) and the Federal Reserve Board to issue jointly regulations requiring financial holding companies subject to stricter standards to develop plans for the rapid and orderly resolution of the company. Prescribes standards for such resolution plans.

Section 1105

Directs the Council to require a financial holding company subject to stricter standards to undertake specified mitigatory actions if the Council determines that the company poses a grave threat to the financial stability or economy of the United States.

Section 1106

Authorizes the Council to subject a financial activity or practice to stricter prudential standards upon a determination that the conduct, scope, nature, size, scale, concentration, or interconnectedness of such activity or practice could create or increase the risk of significant liquidity, credit, or other problems spreading among financial institutions or markets and local, minority, or underserved communities, and thereby threaten the stability of the financial system or economy.

Section 1107

Directs the Federal Reserve Board, as agent of the Council, to recommend to the appropriate primary financial regulatory agencies the prudential standards to be applied to such identified activities and practices.

Section 1108

Requires the Board, when the Council determines that a company or activity or practice no longer is subject to heightened prudential scrutiny, to so inform the relevant primary financial regulatory agency or agencies. Requires the primary financial regulatory agency that has imposed stricter prudential standards for financial stability purposes to determine whether such standards should remain in effect.

Section 1109

Authorizes the FDIC, upon the written determination of the Council that a liquidity event exists that could destabilize the financial system, to create a widely-available program designed to avoid or mitigate adverse effects on systemic economic conditions or financial stability by guaranteeing obligations of solvent insured depository institutions or solvent depository institution holding companies (and affiliates) if necessary to prevent systemic financial instability during times of severe economic distress. Limits to $500 billion the total guaranteed debt outstanding at any time, except in specified circumstances.

Section 1110

Authorizes the FDIC to appoint itself as receiver for an insured depository institution participating in the Sec. 1109 program or another specified debt guarantee program that defaults on any FDIC-guaranteed obligation. Amends the federal bankruptcy code to authorize the FDIC to file an involuntary petition for bankruptcy against a depository institution holding company or another company participating in an FDIC guarantee program on the ground of such a default. Grants a ninth bankruptcy priority to allowed unsecured claims based upon any debt to the FDIC as a result of such default.

Section 1111

Permits the FDIC to obtain warrants or senior debt instruments from an insured depository institution or depository institution holding company in connection with a specified payment, credit extension, or guarantee or any commitment under this Act.

Section 1112

Amends the Federal Deposit Insurance Act (FDIA) to set forth examination and enforcement authority over a financial holding company subject to stricter standards whenever the FDIC Board of Directors determines a special examination is necessary to determine the company's condition for resolution purposes.

Section 1113

Directs the Chairman of the Council to study and report to Congress on the economic impact of possible financial services regulatory limitations intended to reduce systemic risk.

Section 1114

Prohibits any provision of this title relating to the authority of the Federal Reserve Board from being construed as conferring any decision-making authority on presidents of federal reserve banks. Prohibits the Federal Reserve Board from delegating the authority to make any voting decision that the Board is authorized or required to make under this title.

Section 1115

Requires a financial holding company subject to stricter standards to conduct quarterly baseline, adverse, and severely adverse stress tests and report on them to the head of the primary financial regulatory agency and to the Federal Reserve Board. Requires any financial company with over $10 billion in total assets that is not a financial holding company subject to stricter standards to conduct and report on stress tests semiannually.

Section 1116

Authorizes the Federal Reserve Board to promulgate regulations that require a financial holding company subject to stricter standards to maintain a minimum amount of long-term hybrid debt that is convertible to equity upon a Board determination that: (1) the company fails to meet prudential standards;

or (2) threats to the stability of the U.S. Financial system make such a conversion necessary. Directs the Chairman of the Council to study and report to Congress on an optimal implementation of contingent capital requirements to: (1) maximize financial stability, minimize the probability of drawing on the Systemic Resolution Fund (established by this Act) in a financial crisis; and (3) minimize costs for financial holding companies subject to stricter standards.

Section 1117

Authorizes the Federal Reserve Board to prohibit a financial holding company subject to stricter standards from trading certain financial instruments with the company's own money and for its own account (proprietary trading) if the Board determines that such trading threatens either: (1) the safety and soundness of the company; or (2) U.S. Financial stability. Allows the Board to make certain exceptions for proprietary trading ancillary to other company operations if it does not pose a threat to company safety and soundness or to U.S. Financial stability.

Subtitle C - Improvements to Supervision and Regulation of Federal Depository Institutions

Section 1202

Amends the Home Owners' Loan Act (HOLA) to establish a Division of Thrift Supervision within the Office of the Comptroller of the Currency. (Sec. 1203) Amends the Revised Statutes of the United States to direct the Secretary to appoint up to five Deputy Comptrollers of the Currency, including a Senior Deputy Comptroller for National Banks and a Senior Deputy Comptroller for Thrift Supervision. (Sec. 1204) Transfers all functions of the OTS Director to the Office of the Comptroller of the Currency and the new Division of Thrift Supervision, except those relating to the supervision and regulation of - (1) state savings associations, which are transferred to the FDIC; and (2) savings and loan holding companies, which are transferred to the Federal Reserve Board. (Sec. 1207) Abolishes the Office of Thrift Supervision (OTS). (Sec. 1212) Transfers all OTS employees to either the Comptroller of the Currency or the FDIC for employment. (Sec. 1219) Amends the Bank Holding Company Act of 1956 (BHCA) to prescribe procedural requirements for the declaration of dividends by subsidiary savings associations of certain mutual holding companies. Allows a mutual thrift holding company to waive the right to receive such dividends in specified circumstances. (Sec. 1220) Directs the Secretary and the FDIC to submit to Congress and their respective Inspectors General a joint plan for implementing this subtitle. (Sec. 1222) Amends the FDIA, the Alternative Mortgage Transaction Parity Act of 1982, the Bank Holding Company Act of 1956, the Bank Protection Act of 1968, the Bank Service Company Act, the Community Reinvestment Act of 1977, the Depository Institution Management Interlocks Act, the Emergency Homeowners' Relief Act, the Equal Credit Opportunity Act, the Federal Credit Union Act, the Federal Financial Institutions Examination Council Act of 1978, the Federal Home Loan Bank Act, the Federal Reserve Act (FRA), the Financial Institutions Reform, Recovery, and Enforcement Act of 1989, the Housing Act of 1948, the Housing and Community Development Act of 1992, the Housing and Urban-Rural Recovery Act of 1983, the National Housing Act, the Right to Financial Privacy Act of 1978, the Balanced Budget and Emergency Deficit Control Act of 1985 (Gramm-Rudman-Hollings Act), the Crime Control Act of 1990, the Flood Disaster Protection Act of 1973, the Investment Company Act of 1940, the Securities Exchange Act of 1934, and the federal criminal code to reflect the transfer of functions under this subtitle. (Sec. 1255) Amends the International Lending Supervision Act of 1983 to require each appropriate federal banking agency, in establishing capital requirements for banking institutions, to seek to make such requirements countercyclical so that the amount of capital required to be maintained by a banking institution increases in times of economic expansion and decreases in times of economic contraction, consistent with the institution's safety and soundness. (Sec. 1256) Transfers to the Federal Reserve Board all functions of the OTS Director with respect to savings and loan holding companies that are a fraternal beneficiary society or a company that is, together with its affiliates on a consolidated basis, predominantly engaged in the business of insurance. Subtitle D: Further Improvements to the Regulation of Bank Holding Companies and Depository Institutions

Section 1301

Amends the Bank Holding Company Act of 1956 (BHCA) to redefine bank holding company and to prescribe the treatment of industrial loan companies, savings associations, and certain other companies in order to effectuate consolidated supervision of certain financial companies by the Federal Reserve Board. Requires such companies to register as bank holding companies. Requires an entity that is subject to the stricter prudential standards under this Act to establish a special purpose intermediate holding company ("section 6 holding company") if such entity controlled shares or engaged in activities that did not comply with the activity or investment restrictions on financial holding companies prescribed by the Federal Reserve Board. Prescribes restrictions on the activities of such an entity and of a section 6 holding company, including: (1) transactions with affiliates; and (2) certain tying arrangements. Sets forth corporate governance requirements, including one that at least 25% of the members of the board of directors of a section 6 holding company, and each subsidiary of such company, be independent of the parent company of the section 6 holding company and any subsidiary of such parent company. Requires a company that controls a section 6 holding company to serve as a source of financial strength to such subsidiary.

Section 1302

Requires registration with the Federal Reserve Board, within 90 days, of any company that was not a bank holding company the day before enactment of this Act but which becomes one (other than a section 6 holding company) by operation of law upon the enactment of this Act.

Section 1303

Revises requirements for reports to the Board of bank holding companies and subsidiaries. Defines a functionally regulated subsidiary of a bank holding company for report and examination purposes as: (1) an SEC-registered broker or dealer; (2) an SEC-registered investment company; and (3) a futures commission merchant, commodity trading advisor, and commodity pool operator registered with the Commodity Futures Trading Commission (CFTC). Repeals the authority of the Federal Reserve Board to examine functionally regulated subsidiaries of a bank holding company. Requires the Board, however, to use reports of examination of such subsidiaries and of subsidiary depository institutions made by other federal or state regulatory authorities. Repeals the limited authority of the Federal Reserve Board to regulate functionally regulated subsidiaries of bank holding companies.

Section 1304

Requires a bank holding company to be well capitalized and well managed.

Section 1305

Requires a bank holding company to be well capitalized and well managed (currently, only adequately capitalized and adequately managed) to acquire an out-of-state bank. Amends the FDIA to allow the responsible agency to approve an interstate merger transaction only if the resulting bank will continue to be well capitalized and well managed (currently, only adequately capitalized and adequately managed) upon consummation of the transaction.

Section 1306

Amends the FRA to eliminate from the meaning of affiliate any company, including a real estate investment trust, that is sponsored and advised on a contractual basis by the member bank or any subsidiary or affiliate of the member bank. Extends coverage of transactions under the Act to debt obligations (in addition to the acceptance of securities) issued by an affiliate as collateral security for a loan or extension of credit to any person or company. Extends such coverage as well to: (1) any securities borrowing and lending transactions with an affiliate to the extent that the transactions create credit exposure of the member bank to the affiliate; and (2) current and potential future credit exposure to the affiliate on derivative transactions with the affiliate. Repeals the requirement that any collateral (for certain transactions with affiliates) that is subsequently retired or amortized be replaced by additional eligible collateral where needed to keep the percentage of the collateral value relative to the amount of the outstanding loan or extension of credit, guarantee, acceptance, or letter of credit equal to the minimum percentage required at the inception of the transaction. Prohibits the Federal Reserve Board, with respect to a transaction or relationship involving a national bank or federal savings association, from exempting a transaction or relationship from specified requirements unless it obtains the concurrence of the Comptroller of the Currency in addition to obtaining the concurrence of the FDIC Chairman.

Section 1307

Repeals the exemption of covered transactions between a bank and any of its individual financial subsidiaries from the requirement that the aggregate amount of the transaction not exceed 10% of the member bank's capital stock and surplus. Repeals also the exclusion of the financial subsidiary's retained earnings from a bank's investment in one of its individual financial subsidiaries.

Section 1308

Amends the Revised Statutes with respect to the limit of 15% of a national banking association's unimpaired capital and unimpaired surplus on the total loans and extensions of credit it makes to a person outstanding at one time and not fully secured by collateral having a market value at least equal to the amount of the loan or extension of credit. Includes among such loans and extensions of credit the credit exposure to a person arising from a derivative transaction, repurchase agreement, reverse repurchase agreement, securities lending transaction, or securities borrowing transaction between the national banking association and a person. Defines derivative transaction as any transaction that is a contract, agreement, swap, warrant, note, or option based, in whole or in part, on the value of, any interest in, or any quantitative measure or the occurrence of any event relating to, one or more commodities, securities, currencies, interest or other rates, indices, or other assets. Requires the Comptroller of the Currency to prescribe rules with respect to credit exposures arising from any derivative transaction or related agreement or transaction.

Section 1309

Amends the Bank Consolidation and Merger Act, the Revised Statutes, and HOLA to prohibit certain conversions by troubled banks and thrifts between national and state banks and savings associations.

Section 1310

Amends the FRA regarding limits on credit extensions to executive officers, directors, and principal shareholders of member banks (insiders) to declare that a member bank shall be deemed to have extended credit to a person if the member bank has credit exposure to the person arising from a derivative transaction, repurchase agreement, reverse repurchase agreement, securities lending transaction, or securities borrowing transaction between the member bank and the person.

Section 1311

Amends the FDIA to prohibit an insured depository institution from purchasing an asset from, or or selling one to, its executive officers, directors, or principal shareholders unless the transaction is on market terms and, if the transaction represents more than 10% of the institution's capital stock and surplus, the transaction has been approved in advance by a majority of the institution's board of directors (with interested directors not participating).

Section 1312

Amends the BHCA to authorize the Federal Reserve Board to issue regulations relating to the capital levels of bank holding companies.

Section 1313

Amends the BHCA regarding the factors to be considered in deciding whether to approve acquisitions of certain shares by a financial holding company, including both bank and nonbank acquisitions, to require the Federal Reserve Board to consider the extent to which the proposed acquisition, merger, or consolidation may pose risk to the stability of the U.S. Financial system or the U.S. Economy, including the resulting scope, nature, size, scale, concentration, or interconnectedness of activities that are financial in nature. Authorizes Board disapproval of any acquisition, merger, or consolidation of, or by, a financial holding company subject to stricter standards if the Board determines that the resulting concentration of liabilities on a consolidated basis is likely to pose a great threat to financial stability during times of severe economic distress. Allows a financial holding company to commence any nonbanking activity or acquire any nonbanking organization without prior approval of the Board, except for a transaction in which the total assets to be acquired by the financial holding company exceed $25 billion. Amends the FDIA to require the FDIC, when deciding whether to approve a merger, consolidation, or other related transaction between an insured depository institution and a noninsured bank or institution, to take into consideration risk to the stability of the U.S. Financial system or the U.S. Economy, including the resulting scope, nature, size, scale, concentration, or interconnectedness of activities that are financial in nature.

Section 1314

Amends the Securities Exchange Act of 1934 to repeal the statutory framework under which certain investment bank holding companies may elect to become supervised by the Securities Exchange Commission (SEC).

Section 1315

Amends the BHCA to require the Federal Reserve Board or the federal reserve banks to assess fees on bank holding companies with total consolidated assets of $10 billion or more to defray the cost of examining such companies.

Section 1316

Amends the Revised Statutes to authorize the Comptroller of the Currency to charter mutual national banks as bodies corporate existing in perpetuity for the benefit of their depositors and the communities in which they operate. Authorizes such banks to apply to become a federal mutual bank holding company according to a specified procedure.

Section 1317

Amends the FDIA to prohibit the responsible agency (usually the FDIC) from approving an application for an interstate merger transaction if, upon consummation of the transaction, the resulting insured depository institution (including its affiliated insured depository institutions) would control more than 10% of the total amount of deposits of insured depository institutions in the United States. Amends the Home Owners' Loan Act to prohibit the OTS Director now, under this Act, the Federal Reserve Board) from approving a savings and loan holding company's application for an interstate acquisition of a savings association or a savings and loan holding company if the applicant (including its affiliated insured depository institutions) controls, upon consummation of the transaction would control, more than 10% of the total amount of deposits of insured depository institutions in the U.S.

Section 1318

Amends the Revised Statutes and the FDIA to revise requirements for the state "opt-in" election to permit interstate branching through de novo branches. Specifies that the application of a national bank to establish a de novo branch in a state in which the bank does not maintain a branch may be approved if the law of the state where the branch is located, or is to be located, would permit establishment of the branch if the bank were a state bank chartered by such state.

Subtitle E - Improvements to the Federal Deposit Insurance Fund

Section 1401

Amends the FDIA to: (1) redefine "risk-based assessment system" to include consideration of risks posed by affiliates; (2) repeal the provision that no depository institution shall be barred from the lowest-risk category solely because of size; (3) prescribe a formula for determining a risk-focused assessment base; (4) eliminate any mandatory declaration of a dividend if the reserve ratio of the Deposit Insurance Fund (DIF) falls between 1.35% and 1.5% of estimated insured deposits; (5) eliminate the requirement that the FDIC first obtain agreement with the Comptroller of the Currency, and the Federal Reserve Board before requiring any insured depository institution to file additional reports for insurance purposes; (6) eliminate the maximum reserve ratio for the DIF; and (7) require the FDIC to make available to the public, for at least five years, the reserve ratio and the designated reserve ratio using both estimated insured deposits and the assessment base revised under this subtitle.

Subtitle F - Improvements to the Asset-backed Securitization Process

Credit Risk Retention Act of 2009 -

Section 1502

Amends the Securities Act of 1933 to direct the appropriate federal financial regulatory agencies to prescribe regulations to require: (1) any creditor to retain an economic interest in a material portion of the credit risk of any loan the creditor transfers, sells, or conveys to a third party, including for the purpose of including such loan in a pool of loans backing an issuance of asset-backed securities; and (2) any securitizer of asset-backed securities that are backed by certain other assets to retain an economic interest in a material portion of any such asset used to back an issuance of securities. Authorizes such agencies, for certain purposes, to apply such risk retention requirements to credit securitizers in addition to or in substitution (as alternatives) for any or all of the requirements that apply to creditors that make such loans or types of loans. Requires the Federal Reserve Board to study and report to Congress on the combined impact by each individual class of asset-backed security of: (1) the new credit risk retention requirements of this subtitle; and (2) the Financial Accounting Statements 166 and 167 issued by the Financial Accounting Standards Board (FASB).

Section 1503

Amends the Securities Exchange Act of 1934 to authorize the SEC to: (1) provide for the suspension or termination of the duty to file for any class of issuer of asset-backed security; and (2) classify issuers and prescribe requirements appropriate for each class of issuer of asset-backed security. Requires the SEC to prescribe regulations requiring each issuer of an asset-backed security to disclose: (1) information regarding the assets backing each tranche or class of security; and (2) asset-level or loan-level data necessary for investors to independently perform due diligence. Requires asset-level or loan-level data to include unique identifiers relating to loan brokers or originators, the nature and extent of the compensation of the broker or originator of the assets backing the security, and the amount of risk retention of the originator or the securitizer of such assets.

Section 1504

Requires the SEC to prescribe regulations on the use of representations and warranties in the asset-backed securities market that: (1) require credit rating agencies to include in reports accompanying credit ratings a description of the representations, warranties, and enforcement mechanisms available to investors and how they differ from representations, warranties, and enforcement mechanisms in similar issuances; and (2) require disclosure on fulfilled repurchase requests across all trusts aggregated by originator, so that investors may identify asset originators with clear underwriting deficiencies.

Section 1505

Amends the Securities Act of 1933 to repeal the exemption from prohibitions and requirements relating to interstate commerce and the mails that is granted to certain transactions involving offers or sales of promissory notes secured by a first lien on real estate upon which is located a residential or commercial structure. .

Section 1506

Requires the Chairman of the Council to study and report to Congress on the macroeconomic effects of the risk retention requirements under this subtitle, emphasizing the potential beneficial effects with respect to stabilizing the real estate market.

Subtitle G - Enhanced Dissolution Authority

Dissolution Authority for Large, Interconnected Financial Companies Act of 2009 -

Section 1603

Sets forth circumstances under which: (1) the Federal Reserve Board or the appropriate regulatory agency (the FDIC, the SEC, or the applicable state insurance authority) is required or authorized to make a written recommendation regarding the systemic risk to U.S. economic stability posed by a financial company in default or in danger of default (covered financial company); and (2) the Secretary shall appoint the FDIC as receiver for such company for a one-year period to take certain discretionary actions to stabilize or dissolve it. Establishes the Systemic Dissolution Fund to: (1) provide for the dissolution of any failed covered financial company (or companies) posing a systemic threat to either the financial markets or to the economy; and (2) ensure that taxpayer funds used to facilitate such liquidations are fully repaid from assessments levied on financial companies with assets of $50 billion or more.

Section 1611

Requires the Inspector General of the FDIC, if the FDIC is appointed as receiver for a covered financial company under this subtitle, to establish an Office of Dissolution, headed by a Special Deputy Inspector General for Dissolution. Requires the Special Deputy Inspector General to audit and investigate the activities of the FDIC in its capacity as receiver for a covered financial company. Requires an Office of Dissolution to terminate six months after the FDIC ceases to serve as a receiver for any covered financial company.

Section 1612

Amends federal bankruptcy law to require that an involuntary case in bankruptcy be commenced by the FDIC against a covered financial company. Requires that the FDIC be appointed trustee in such a case.

Section 1613

Amends the FDIA to require the FDIC to establish a Systemic Dissolution Authority, which shall manage any fund established for the purpose of facilitating the dissolution of a financial company (Systemic Dissolution Fund).

Section 1614

Requires the FDIC to apply specified executive compensation limits under the Emergency Economic Stabilization Act of 2008 (EESA) to a covered financial company, for so long as it is in receivership, at any time that the FDIC has borrowed from the Treasury to resolve the company.

Section 1615

Directs Comptroller General to study and report to Congress on the safe harbor provisions under federal law for derivatives, swaps, and securities transactions, including recommendations for legislation to address any adverse impacts presented by such provisions.

Section 1616

Directs the Secretary to study and report to Congress on how the resolution authority provided under this subtitle should be funded.

Section 1617

Amends the FDIA with respect to the order of priority for payment of claims from amounts realized from the liquidation or other resolution of any insured depository institution by any receiver. Grants third priority to any obligation of the institution owed to the FDIC as a result of the institution's default on a FDIC-guaranteed debt.

Subtitle H - Additional Improvements for Financial Crisis Management

Section 1701

Amends the Federal Reserve Act (FRA) to empower the Federal Reserve Board, in unusual and exigent circumstances, to authorize any federal reserve bank to discount certain notes, drafts, and bills of exchange (except low quality assets) upon the written determination of the Financial Stability Oversight Council (with the consent of the Secretary) that an existing liquidity event could destabilize the financial system. Requires the Financial Stability Oversight Council to promptly notify Congress of its determination. Sets a ceiling of $4 trillion upon the availability of such amounts. Authorizes introduction and passage in Congress of a joint resolution disapproving any additional borrowing authority under this subtitle.

Section 1702

Subjects the exercise of a federal reserve bank's foreign currency swap authority to advance approval by at least five members of the Federal Reserve Board and the written concurrence of the Secretary of the Treasury.

Section 1703

Establishes the Council of Inspectors General on Financial Oversight.

Subtitle I - Miscellaneous

Section 1801

Directs each financial regulatory agency to establish an Office of Minority and Women Inclusion to advise the agency administrator on the impact of agency policies and regulations upon minority-owned and women-owned businesses.

Section 1802

Amends the Federal Financial Institutions Examination Council Act of 1987 to require the Federal Housing Finance Agency (FHFA) to participate in an advisory role whenever the Financial Institutions Examination Council takes any actions on issues relating to either the Federal National Mortgage

Association (Fannie Mae), the Federal Home Loan Mortgage Corporation (Freddie Mac), or the federal home loan banks.

Subtitle J - International Policy Coordination

Section 1901

Directs the President (or a designee) to coordinate through all available international policy channels similar policies as found in U.S. law related to limiting the scope, nature, size, scale, concentration, and interconnectedness of financial companies in order to protect financial stability and the global economy.

Subtitle K - International Financial Provisions

Section 1951

Amends the International Banking Act of 1978 to authorize the Federal Reserve Board, in acting on any application for the establishment of a foreign bank office in the United States, to take into account for a foreign bank that presents a systemic risk to the United States, whether the home country of the foreign bank has adopted, or is making demonstrable progress toward adopting, an appropriate system of financial regulation for the home country financial system to mitigate such systemic risk. Authorizes the Federal Reserve Board to terminate the activities of a branch, agency, or subsidiary of a foreign bank operating in the United States if the Board finds that the home country of a foreign bank that presents a systemic risk to the United States has neither adopted nor made demonstrable progress toward adopting an appropriate system of financial regulation to mitigate systemic risk. Amends the Securities Exchange Act of 1934 to authorize the SEC, when determining whether to permit or terminate registration of a foreign person as a U.S. broker or dealer, to consider whether, for a foreign person (or affiliate) that presents a systemic risk to the United States, the foreign person's home country has either adopted or made demonstrable progress toward adopting an appropriate system of financial regulation to mitigate systemic risk. Authorizes the SEC to terminate the broker or dealer registration of a foreign person whose home country has not adopted or made progress toward adopting an appropriate system of financial regulation.

Section 1952

Amends the Emergency Economic Stabilization Act of 2008 (EESA) to modify the amount by which Troubled Asset Relief Program (TARP) funds authorized for purchase of troubled assets are reduced to offset costs. Increases the amount by which $700 billion must be reduced to $23.625 billion.

Subtitle L - Securities Holding Companies

Section 1961

Prescribes requirements for U.S. registration and supervision, including capital and risk management, of certain securities holding companies required by a foreign regulator or foreign law to be subject to comprehensive consolidated supervision.

TITLE II - CORPORATE AND FINANCIAL INSTITUTION COMPENSATION FAIRNESS ACT

Corporate and Financial Institution Compensation Fairness Act of 2009 -

Section 2002

Amends the Securities Exchange Act of 1934 to require that any proxy, consent, or authorization to elect directors for an annual shareholders meeting provide for a separate shareholder vote to approve executive compensation in accordance with SEC rules. States that the shareholder vote shall not be binding upon the issuer or the board of directors. Requires the person making a proxy or consent solicitation to approve at a shareholders meeting of an acquisition, merger, consolidation, or proposed sale or other disposition of all or substantially all the assets of an issuer to disclose in the related material any agreements or understandings that such person has with any named executive officers of such issuer or of the acquiring issuer concerning all compensation based upon or relating to such asset disposition, and the aggregate total of all such compensation that may be paid or become payable to or on behalf of such executive officer (golden parachute compensation).

Section 2003

Requires the SEC to direct the national securities exchanges and associations to prohibit the listing of any class of equity security of an issuer that is not in compliance with specified SEC standards relating to compensation committees, including: (1) the independence of such committees; (2) independence standards for compensation consultants and other committee advisors; and (3) compensation committee authority relating to compensation consultants.

Section 2004

Directs federal regulators to prescribe joint regulations requiring certain financial institutions to disclose the structures of all incentive-based compensation arrangements offered by them in order to determine whether the compensation structure: (1) is aligned with sound risk management; (2) is structured to account for the time horizon of risks; and (3) meets other criteria appropriate to reduce unreasonable incentives offered by such institutions for employees to take undue risks that could threaten the safety and soundness of covered financial institutions or have serious adverse effects on economic conditions or financial stability. Requires federal regulators to prescribe joint regulations prohibiting any feature of any incentive-based arrangement that encourages such inappropriate risks. Exempts financial institutions with assets of less than $1 billion from such compensation prohibitions and requirements. Requires the Comptroller to study and report to Congress on whether there is a correlation between compensation structures and excessive risk taking.

TITLE III - DERIVATIVE MARKETS TRANSPARENCY AND ACCOUNTABILITY ACT

Derivative Markets Transparency and Accountability Act of 2009 -

Section 3001

Directs the Commodity Futures Trading Commission (CFTC) and the SEC to consult with one another and with the Prudential Regulators before commencing any rulemaking or issuing an order regarding swaps, swap dealers, major swap participants, swap repositories, persons associated with a swap dealer or major swap participant, eligible contract participants, or swap execution facilities.

Section 3003

Requires the CFTC, the SEC, and the Prudential Regulators to consult and coordinate with foreign regulatory authorities on the establishment of consistent international standards for the regulation of contracts of sale of swaps and security-based swaps. Authorizes the CFTC, the SEC, and the Prudential Regulators to agree to information-sharing arrangements necessary or appropriate in the public interest, or for the protection of investors, swap counterparties, and security-based swap counterparties. Requires the CFTC to consult and coordinate with foreign regulatory authorities on the establishment of consistent international standards with respect to the regulation of contracts of sale of a commodity for future delivery. Permits the CFTC to agree with foreign regulatory authorities on information-sharing arrangements necessary or appropriate in the public interest for the protection users of contracts of sale of a commodity for future delivery.

Section 3004

Prohibits this Act from being construed as authorizing federal assistance to support clearing operations or liquidation of a derivatives clearing organization or a clearing agency, except where explicitly authorized by an Act of Congress.

Section 3005

Requires the CFTC to study and report to Congress regarding the effects of the position limits imposed under this title on excessive speculation and on the movement of transactions from exchanges in the United States to trading venues outside the United States. Instructs the Chairman of the CFTC to report biennially to Congress on the growth or decline of the derivatives markets in the United States and abroad. Directs the CFTC and the SEC to study jointly and report to certain congressional committees on: (1) the feasibility of requiring the derivatives industry to adopt standardized computer-readable algorithmic descriptions which may be used to describe complex and standardized financial derivatives; and (2) the desirability and feasibility of establishing, by January 1, 2012, a single regulator for all transactions involving financial derivatives.

Section 3006

Directs the CFTC, the SEC, and the Prudential Regulators to transmit to Congress recommendations for legislative changes to the federal insolvency laws.

Section 3007

Authorizes the CFTC and the SEC jointly to collect information concerning the markets for any types of swap or security-based swap and and issue a report on those detrimental to the stability of a financial market or of its participants.

Section 3008

Authorizes either the CFTC or the SEC to prohibit an entity domiciled in a foreign country from participating in the United States in any swap or security-based swap activities if the regulation of swaps or security-based swaps markets in that foreign country undermines the stability of the U.S. Financial system.

Section 3009

Directs the CFTC and the Federal Energy Regulatory Commission (FERC) to negotiate and submit to Congress a memorandum of understanding to establish procedures for: (1) applying their respective authorities in a manner to ensure effective regulation in the public interest; (2) resolving conflicts concerning overlapping jurisdiction between the two agencies; (3) avoiding conflicting or duplicative regulation; and (4) sharing information where either Commission is investigating potential manipulation, fraud, or market power abuse in markets within its purview.

Subtitle A - Regulation of Swap Markets

Section 3102

Amends the Commodity Exchange Act (CEA) with respect to CFTC exclusive jurisdiction over accounts, agreements and transactions involving swaps, and contracts of sale executed on a swaps execution facility. States that such CFTC jurisdiction limits neither the jurisdiction conferred by this Act upon the SEC with respect to security-based swap agreements and security-based swaps, nor SEC authority with respect to related agreements, contracts, or transactions. States that CFTC jurisdiction does not limit or affect the authority of FERC with respect to agreements, contracts, or transactions: (1) not executed, traded, or cleared on a registered entity or trading facility; and (2) entered into pursuant to a FERC-approved tariff or rate schedule.

Section 3103

Repeals the exclusion from regulation of certain derivative transactions, electronic trading facilities, swap transactions, and transactions in exempt commodities. Requires submission of a swap for clearing if a registered derivatives clearing organization will accept it for clearing and the CFTC determines that the swap is required to be cleared. Requires the CFTC to review each swap, or any group, category, type or class of swaps to make a determination as to whether it should be required to be cleared.

States it shall be unlawful for any person, other than an eligible contract participant, to enter into that a swap unless the swap is entered into on or subject to the rules of a board of trade designated as a contract market under the CEA. Extends registration requirements to derivatives clearing organizations with respect to swaps. Requires the CFTC to adopt rules forthe clearing by a derivatives clearing organization of a swap, or a group, category, type or class of swaps. Sets forth reporting requirements for swaps that are not accepted for clearing by any derivatives clearing organization. Prohibits a swap that is subject to the clearing requirement of this Act from being traded except on or through a board of trade designated as a contract market under this Act, or on or through a swap execution facility registered under this Act that makes the swap available for trading. Modifies registration requirements governing derivatives clearing organizations, including governing core principles, risk management,and reporting requirements. Requires each derivatives clearing organization to designate an individual to serve as a compliance officer. Amends the Legal Certainty for Bank Products Act of 2000 to state that, subject to certain exceptions, the CEA shall not apply to, and the CFTC shall not exercise regulatory authority under such Act with respect to, an identified banking product.

Section 3104

Amends the CEA to require the CFTC to make available to the public from derivatives clearing organizations, swap repositories, and other specified reports aggregate data on swap trading volumes and positions, in a manner that does not disclose the business transactions and market positions of any person.

Section 3105

Prohibits any person, unless registered with the CFTC, from making use of the mails or any means or instrumentality of interstate commerce to perform the functions of a swap repository. Requires a swap repository to accept, maintain, and provide to the CFTC and other specified federal banking agencies data the CFTC prescribes for each swap.

Section 3106

Sets forth reporting and recordkeeping requirements for certain swaps.

Section 3107

Subjects swap dealers, major swap participants, and swap execution facilities to requirements for registration, regulation, and conflicts of interest.

Section 3110

Amends the CEA to repeal current requirements for derivatives transaction execution facilities and an election for registration by exempt boards of trade. Permits an exempt board of trade to petition the CFTC to remain subject to such requirements, however, for one year after the effective date of this subtitle.

Section 3111

Revises requirements for a board of trade which has been designated as a contract market. Requires such a board of trade to: (1) have adequate financial, operational, and managerial resources to discharge contract market responsibilities; (2) establish a program of risk analysis and oversight to identify and minimize sources of operational risk; (3) establish emergency procedures, backup facilities, and a plan for disaster recovery; (4) conduct periodic tests to verify that back-up resources are sufficient to ensure continued order processing and trade matching, price reporting, market surveillance, and maintenance of a comprehensive and accurate audit trail; and (5) establish and enforce disciplinary procedures. Requires the board of directors of a publicly traded board of trade recruit individuals from a broad and culturally diverse pool of qualified candidates.

Section 3112

Repeals the current prohibition to authorize the CFTC to regulate the setting of levels of margin for an registered entity.

Section 3113

Directs the CFTC to establish position limits on: (1) trading or positions held by any group or class of traders; and (2) positions (other than bona fide hedge positions) that may be held by any person with respect to either contracts of sale for future delivery, or options on contracts or commodities traded on or subject to the rules of a designated contract market.

Section 3114

Repeals the current prohibition to permit a CFTC interpretation issued with respect to significant price discovery contracts to provide the exclusive means for complying with acceptable business practices. Includes swap execution facilities within registered entities subject to CFTC interpretations.

Section 3115

Prohibits the CFTC from permitting a foreign board of trade to provide its members or other participants located in the United States with direct access to its electronic trading and order-matching system with respect to an agreement, contract, or transaction that settles against any price of contracts listed for trading on a registered entity, unless the Commission makes specified findings.

Section 3116

Revises the denial of voidability of hybrid instruments, transactions, and contracts based solely on any failure to comply with CFTC terms or conditions. Extends such denial to the voidability of agreement, contract, or transaction between eligible contract participants (or persons reasonably believed to be such) based solely on the failure of the agreement, contract, or transaction to meet the CFTC definition of a swap.

Section 3117

Amends the Federal Deposit Insurance Corporation Improvement Act of 1991 to repeal its coverage of multilateral clearing organizations.

Section 3118

Grants the CFTC exclusive enforcement authority over swap markets. Grants the Prudential Regulators exclusive authority to enforce certain prudential requirements with respect to banks as well as branches or agencies of foreign banks that are swap dealers or major swap participants. Authorizes the CFTC and the Prudential Regulators to refer noncompliance with the other's requirements to the other. Declares specified disruptive practices unlawful.

Section 3119

Amends the FDIA to subject any swap dealer, major swap participant, security-based swap dealer, major security-based swap participant, derivatives clearing organization, swap repository, security-based swap repository, or swap execution facility, whether or not it is an insured depository institution, to the cease-and-desist authority of the Federal Reserve Board, the FDIC, or the Office of the Comptroller of the Currency, as appropriate.

Section 3120

Amends the CEA to: (1) grant the CFTC jurisdiction over specified retail commodity transactions; (2) require large swap traders to make specified reports and disclosures to the CFTC; and (3) require segregation of a counterparty's assets to be held as collateral in over-the-counter swap transactions not submitted for clearing to a derivatives clearing organization.

Subtitle B - Regulation of Security-Based Swap Markets

Section 3202

Amends the Gramm-Leach-Bliley Act to repeal the prohibition against regulation of a security-based swap agreement.

Section 3203

Amends the Securities Exchange Act of 1934 to prescribe requirements for clearing procedures and execution of security-based swaps, including requirements for: (1) swap execution facilities; (2) segregation of assets held as collateral in security-based swap transactions; (3) position limits and accountability for security-based swaps and large trader reporting; (4) registration and regulation of security-based swap dealers and major security-based swap participants; and (5) reporting and recordkeeping for certain security-based swaps. Requires a clearing agency to submit and the SEC to review each security-based swap, or any group, category, type or class of security-based swaps to determine whether it should be required to be cleared.

Section 3206

Modifies the application of state gaming and bucket shop laws to declare inapplicable to any transaction in a security-based swap, including one effected on a registered national securities exchange, any state law which prohibits or regulates the making or promoting of wagering or gaming contracts, or the operation of bucket shops or other similar or related activities. Prohibits a security-based swap from being regulated under state law as an insurance contract.

Section 3207

Amends the Securities Exchange Act of 1933 to set forth the registration requirements for certain security-based swaps, as well for the exemption of certain other security-based swaps from registration requirements.

Subtitle C - Improved Financial and Commodity Markets Oversight and Accountability

Section 3301

Amends the Inspector General Act of 1978 to require the heads of designated federal agencies, including the Federal Reserve Board, the CFTC, and the SEC (covered establishments), to each: (1) take action to address deficiencies identified by a report or investigation of the agency Inspector General; or (2) certify to both Houses of Congress that no action is necessary or appropriate in connection with certain deficiencies.

Section 3305

Amends the CEA to authorize the CFTC to define "commercial risk," "operating risk," and "balance sheet risk."

Section 3306

Requires the rules of a derivatives clearing organization or a swap execution facility that clears swaps to prohibit: (1) specified owners ("restricted owners") from being permitted to acquire beneficial ownership of interests in the organization or in persons with a controlling interest in the organization or in the facility, to the extent that such an acquisition would result in restricted owners being entitled to vote, cause the voting of, or cause the withholding of votes of more than 20% of the votes entitled to be cast by the holders of the ownership interests; and (2) a majority of the directors of the organization or of the facility from being associated with a restricted owner. Requires a board of trade to establish and enforce rules to minimize conflicts of interest in the decisionmaking process of a contract market, and establish a process for resolving any such conflicts. Requires the rules of a board of trade that trades swaps to make similar conflicts of interest prohibitions for restricted owners as well as its own directors.

TITLE IV - CONSUMER FINANCIAL PROTECTION AGENCY ACT

Consumer Financial Protection Agency Act of 2009 -

Subtitle A - Establishment of the Agency

Section 4101

Establishes the Consumer Financial Protection Agency (Agency) to regulate consumer financial products or services, led by a Director until the Agency conversion date.

Section 4103

Creates a Commission to succeed to all the authorities of the Agency after the specified conversion date.

Section 4104

Establishes the Consumer Financial Protection Oversight Board, composed of the senior executives of specified financial institution regulatory agencies to advise the Director.

Section 4106

Requires the Director to establish: (1) an Office of Financial Literacy; (2) an Office of Financial Protection for Older Americans; and (3) an Office of Fair Lending and Equal Opportunity. Prohibits the Director of the Office of Fair Lending and Equal Opportunity from allowing a covered organization to participate in any program established by the Office. Directs the Agency to establish: (1) a single, toll-free telephone number for consumer complaints and inquiries concerning institutions the federal financial institution regulatory agencies regulate; (2) a system for collecting and monitoring such complaints; and (3) a system for routing such calls to the federal agency that primarily supervises the financial institution, or that is otherwise the appropriate federal agency to address the subject of the complaint or inquiry.

Section 4107

Requires the Director to establish a Consumer Advisory Board.

Section 4108

Requires the Director to: (1) coordinate with specified federal agencies and state regulators to promote consistent regulatory treatment and enforcement of consumer and investment products, services, and laws; and (2) submit to Congress a periodic annual status report.

Section 4110

Directs the Comptroller to study and report periodically to Congress on the effects of Agency regulations upon small businesses.

Section 4111

Directs the Federal Reserve Board to transfer specified funds annually to the Director to implement this Act. Prescribes assessment procedures for depository institutions covered persons and nondepository institution covered persons. (A covered person is, except for certain federal officers and federal agencies or bureaus, any person who engages directly or indirectly in a financial activity in connection with the provision of a consumer financial product or service.) Authorizes appropriations for FY2010-FY2014. Establishes in the Treasury: (1) the Consumer Financial Protection Agency Depository Institution Fund (CFPA Depository Fund); (2) the Consumer Financial Protection Agency Nondepository Institution Fund (CFPA Nondepository Fund); and (3) the Consumer Financial Protection Agency Civil Penalty Fund (for payments to victims of activities for which civil penalties have been imposed). Amends the Housing and Economic Recovery Act of 2008 to: (1) revise requirements for grants for financial education and counseling services to make them services to individuals at financial risk (currently, to prospective homebuyers); and (2) instruct the Agency Director to establish criteria for determining whether an individual is at financial risk.

Cites conditions exempting a nondepository institution covered person from Agency assessments.

Section 4113

Authorizes the Comptroller General to audit Agency programs, activities, receipts, expenditures, and financial transactions.

Subtitle B - General Powers of the Director and Agency

Section 4201

Requires the Director to seek to promote transparency, simplicity, fairness, accountability, and equal access in the market for consumer financial products or services.

Section 4202

Sets forth the general oversight and enforcement powers of the Director and the Agency, including coordination of supervisory actions with other agencies and the examination and enforcement for small banks, thrifts, and credit unions.

Section 4203

Requires the appropriate federal banking agency, for insured depository institutions with total assets of $10 billion or less, or the National Credit Union Administration (NCUA), for insured credit unions with total assets of $10 billion or less, periodically to examine, or require reports from, such an institution to ensure and enforce compliance with the requirements of this title, specified consumer laws, and any regulation prescribed by the Director. Establishes in the Agency the Assistive

Division for Community Financial Institutions to - (1) advise the Director on the impact of Agency policies and regulations on community financial institutions; and (2) help ensure that Agency policies and regulations do not unduly burden community financial institutions. (Sec. 4204) Requires a federal banking agency and the Agency, with respect to each insured depository institution, credit union, or other covered person supervised by the federal banking agency and the Agency, respectively, to: (1) coordinate the scheduling of examinations of the insured depository institution, and credit union, or other covered person; (2) conduct

simultaneous examinations of each insured depository institution, credit union or other covered person, unless such institution requests examinations to be conducted separately; (3) share each draft report of examination with the other agency and permit the receiving agency a reasonable opportunity to comment on the draft report before such report is made final; and (4) before issuing a final report of examination or taking supervisory action, take into consideration concerns, if any, raised in the comments made by the other agency. Requires the Agency to pursue arrangements and agreements with state bank supervisors to coordinate such examinations. Authorizes an insured depository institution, credit union, or other covered person, if the proposed material supervisory determinations of the Agency and a federal banking agency are conflicting, to request the agencies to coordinate and present a joint statement of coordinated supervisory action. Prescribes requirements for composition of a governing panel to hear an appeal of an insured depository institution, credit union, or other covered person if: (1) such a joint statement is not issued: or (2) either agency takes or attempts to take any supervisory action relating to the request for the joint statement without the other agency's consent. (Sec. 4205) Prohibits the Director and the Agency from exercising any rulemaking, supervisory, enforcement authority (including authority to order assessments) with respect to: (1) credit extended directly by a merchant, retailer, or seller of nonfinancial goods or services to a consumer, if such good or service is not itself a consumer financial product or service, exclusively for the purpose of enabling the purchase such goods or services directly from the merchant, retailer, or seller of nonfinancial services; or (2) collection of debt, directly by the merchant, retailer, or seller of nonfinancial services, arising from such extension of credit. Excludes from the regulatory authority of the Director and the Agency any person regulated by the SEC, the CFTC, a state securities commission, a state insurance regulator, the FHFA, the Farm Credit Administration, employee benefit and compensation plans, , accountants and tax preparers, real estate licensees, auto dealers, manufactured home retailers and modular home retailers, pawnbrokers, certain consumer reporting agencies, as well as certain activities related to charitable contributions or engaged in by an attorney as part of a law practice. Prohibits this title from being construed to confer authority on the Director or the Agency to establish a usury limit applicable to an extension of credit offered or made by a covered person to a consumer. (Sec. 4207) Requires the Agency to monitor for risks to consumers in the

provision of consumer financial products or services, including developments in markets for such products or services. Requires the Agency to conduct an assessment of each significant regulation prescribed or order issued by the Director. (Sec. 4208) Authorizes the Director to restrict mandatory predispute arbitration. (Sec. 4209) Requires the Agency to: (1) develop risk-based programs to supervise covered persons that are not credit unions, depository institutions, or specified persons excluded under Section 4205; and (2) prescribe regulations regarding registration requirements for covered persons that are not credit unions or depository institutions. Subtitle C: Specific Authorities

Section 4301

Authorizes the Agency to: (1) prohibit unfair, deceptive, or abusive acts or practices in connection with any transaction or offering of a consumer financial product or service; and (2) prescribe regulations to ensure timely, appropriate, and effective disclosures to consumers of the costs, benefits, and risks associated with any consumer financial product or service, as well as the manner, settings, and circumstances for the provision (sale) of such products or services.

Section 4304

Requires the Agency to establish standards and procedures for approval of pilot disclosures to be made by a covered person to consumers in connection with a consumer financial product or service.

Section 4305

Encourages the states to prescribe standards applicable to covered persons who are not insured depository institutions or credit unions, or service providers, to deter and detect unfair, deceptive, abusive, fraudulent, or illegal transactions in the provision of consumer financial products or services. Authorizes the Director to prescribe regulations for minimum standards, including registration or licensing standards, for any class of covered persons other than those subject to the jurisdiction of a federal banking agency or a state bank supervisor, or for any service provider.

Section 4306

Requires the Director to prescribe: (1) regulations imposing duties on covered persons (or their employees, agents, or contractors) who deal or communicate directly with consumers in the provision of a consumer financial product or service; and (2) standards applicable to covered persons to promote standardized formats for information to be made available to consumers.

Section 4308

Specifies prohibited acts related to: (1) the marketing or enforcement of the terms of a consumer financial product; (2) failure or refusal to pay Agency-imposed fees or assessments; and (3) knowing or reckless assistance to others in violation of the requirements of this Act.

Section 4309

Prescribes mandatory disclosures for remittance transfers. Directs the Federal Reserve Board to work with the federal reserve banks to expand the use of the automated clearinghouse system for remittance transfers to foreign countries. Instructs the Director to report to the President and certain congressional committees on the feasibility of and impediments to use of remittance history in calculation of a consumer's credit score.

Section 4311

Prohibits the Director from prescribing any regulation, issuing any order or guidance, or taking any other action, including any enforcement action, the effect of which would be to require a covered person to offer to any consumer a specific financial product or service.

Section 4312

Requires the Director to: (1) lead a Negotiated Rulemaking Committee to promulgate certain appraisal independence requirements for residential loans; (2) promulgate a new rule requiring banks to place prominently in each consumer branch office information regarding the fees and charges associated with enrollment in the bank's overdraft protection program; and (3) review federal laws and regulations relating to the protection of persons who utilize exchange facilitators, and report to Congress any recommendations to ensure protection of persons who utilize exchange facilitators.

Section 4315

Amends the Securities Act of 1933 to exempt from its coverage any consumer loan, and any note representing a whole or fractional interest in any such loan, funded or sold through a person-to-person lending platform

(Internet website). Confers upon the Agency primary jurisdiction for the regulation of the lending activities of person-to-person lending and related platforms.

Section 4316

Requires the Director to prescribe regulations identifying any acts or practices as unlawful, unfair, deceptive, or abusive in connection with a reverse mortgage transaction or the offering of a reverse mortgage.

Subtitle D - Preservation of State Law

Section 4401

Declares that this Act shall not be construed as annulling, altering, or affecting, or exempting any person subject to this title from complying with state law, except to the extent of any inconsistency with this Act. Declares that state law and regulations that afford consumers greater protection than that provided under this Act are not inconsistent with this Act. Requires the Agency to: (1) issue a notice of proposed rulemaking whenever a majority of the states has enacted a resolution in support of the establishment or modification of a consumer protection regulation by the Agency; and (2) take specified considerations into account before prescribing a final regulation based upon such notice (including whether the proposed regulation would afford greater protection to consumers than any existing regulation).

Section 4402

Authorizes a state attorney general to bring a civil action in the name of the state in federal or state court to enforce and secure remedies under this Act. Affirms the authority of: (1) state securities regulators and state insurance regulators to take action with respect to a person regulated by them; and (2) the Comptroller of the Currency and the Director of the Office of Thrift Supervision (OTS) [sic] regarding the applicability of state law under federal banking law to existing contracts entered into by the national banks and federal savings associations within their regulatory purview.

Section 4404

Amends the Revised Statutes and the Home Owners' Loan Act to prescribe state law preemption standards and visitorial standards for national banks, federal savings associations, and nondepository institution subsidiaries.

Subtitle E - Enforcement Powers

Section 4502

Sets forth Agency enforcement powers, including those for investigations, adjudication and litigation authority. Prohibits this Act from being construed as: (1) creating a private right of action; or (2) denying any private right of action arising under specified consumer laws.

Subtitle F - Transfer of Functions and Personnel; Transitional Provisions

Section 4601

Transfers from the following entities to the Director certain consumer financial protection functions: (1) the Federal Reserve Board; (2) the Comptroller of the Currency; (3) the OTS Director; (4) the FDIC; (5) the Federal Trade Commission (FTC); (6) NCUA; and (7) the Secretary of Housing and Urban Development (HUD) (relating to the Real Estate Settlement Procedures Act of 1974 and the Secure and Fair Enforcement for Mortgage Licensing Act of 2008).

Section 4604

Provides for the transfer of affected personnel.

Subtitle G - Regulatory Improvements

Section 4701

Requires financial institutions to maintain records of the number and dollar amounts of deposit accounts of their customers for each branch, automated teller machine (ATM) at which deposits are accepted, and other deposit taking service facility.

Section 4702

Amends the Equal Credit Opportunity Act to require each financial institution, in the case of an application for credit for a small business, to: (1) inquire whether the business is a women- or minority-owned business; and (2) maintain a separate record of the responses to such inquiry. Restricts access to such information by loan underwriters or other employees of the financial institution. Requires such information to be compiled and maintained by each financial institution and submitted annually to the Agency, which shall make it available for public disclosure.

Section 4703

Requires the Director to report annually to Congress on foreclosures and bankruptcies during the previous calendar year, including: (1) their underlying causes; and (2) specific financial products or services causing substantial numbers of such bankruptcies or foreclosures and the companies or individuals which provided them.

Section 4704

Amends the Helping Families Save Their Homes Act of 2009 to direct the Comptroller of the Currency and the OTS [sic] Director to collect and report certain mortgage modification data as it pertains to each state.

Subtitle H - Conforming Amendments

Makes conforming amendments to specified Acts to reflect the provisions of this Act.

Subtitle I - Improvements to the Federal Trade Commission Act

Section 4901

Amends the Federal Trade Commission Act (FTCA) to declare it unlawful for any person, partnership, or corporation to knowingly or recklessly provide substantial assistance to another in violating any provision of the FTCA or of any other Act enforceable by the FTC that relates to unfair or deceptive acts or practices.

Subtitle J - Miscellaneous

Section 4951

Amends the S.A.F.E. Mortgage Licensing Act of 2008 to authorize a state loan originator supervisory authority to review applicants and grant, on a case-by-case basis, exceptions to the minimum standard governing state-licensed loan originators.

TITLE V - CAPITAL MARKETS

Subtitle A - Private Fund Investment Advisers Registration Act

Private Fund Investment Advisers Registration Act of 2009 -

Section 5003

Amends the Investment Advisers Act of 1940 to repeal its exemption and apply registration requirements to a private fund investment adviser. Exempts from investment adviser registration requirements: (1) a foreign private fund adviser; (2) CFTC-registered commodity trading advisors whose business does not consist primarily of acting as an investment adviser, and that do not act as investment advisers to a private fund; or (3) an investment adviser who solely advises specified small business entities.

Section 5004

Subjects to SEC recordkeeping requirements any registered investment adviser who advises private funds. Authorizes the SEC to make such records, especially those relating to systemic risk, available to the Federal Reserve Board and the Financial Services Oversight Council.

Section 5005

Repeals the declaration that no provision of such Act shall be construed to require, or to authorize the SEC to require, any investment adviser engaged in rendering investment supervisory services to disclose the identity, investments, or affairs of any client, except insofar as disclosure may be necessary or appropriate in a particular proceeding or investigation having as its object the enforcement of such Act.

Section 5006

Requires the SEC to exempt from the registration requirements of this Act any venture capital fund advisers and any private fund adviser that acts solely as an adviser to private funds and has assets under management in the United States of less than $150 million. Directs the SEC to require the latter advisers, however, to maintain records and make annual reports to the SEC.

Section 5007

Directs the SEC, with respect to investment advisers acting as investment advisers to mid-sized private funds, to: (1) take into account the size, governance, and investment strategy of such funds to determine whether they pose systemic risk; and (2) provide for registration and examination procedures with respect to the investment advisers of such funds which reflect the level of systemic risk such funds pose.

Section 5008

Modifies SEC rulemaking authority. Instructs the SEC and the CFTC to promulgate rules jointly for required reports filed by certain registered investment advisers.

Section 5009

Directs the Comptroller General to assess and report to Congress on the annual costs on industry members and their investors due to the registration requirements and ongoing reporting requirements under this Act.

Subtitle B - Accountability and Transparency in Rating Agencies Act

Accountability and Transparency in Rating Agencies Act of 2009 -

Section 6002

Amends the Securities Exchange Act of 1934 to exempt from the requirement that each credit rating agency register as a nationally recognized statistical rating organization (NRSRO) any credit rating agency that: (1) does not engage in the provision of credit ratings to securities issuers for a fee; and (2) issues credit ratings only in any bona fide newspaper, news magazine, or business or financial publication of general and regular circulation. Exempts as well any other persons which the SEC may designate when in the public interest and for the protection of investors.

Directs the SEC to examine credit ratings issued by each NRSRO to determine whether the NRSRO has established and documented internal processes for determining credit ratings consistent with SEC rules. Requires each NRSRO to make available and maintain such records and information as the SEC may prescribe for such examinations. Requires the SEC to prescribe specified rules governing NRSRO disclosures of procedures and methodologies used to determine the credit ratings of structured securities, including disclosure on a publicly accessible Internet site, in a central database, of the historical default rates of all classes of financial products rated by an NRSRO. Modifies SEC powers to impose fines and censure a noncompliant NRSRO, including NRSRO failure to: (1) guard against certain violations; and (2) conduct sufficient surveillance to ensure that credit ratings remain current. Conditions the general authorization for an NRSRO to withdraw from registration upon its certification that it received less than $250 million during its last full fiscal year in net revenue for providing credit ratings on securities and money market instruments issued in the United States. Prescribes rules for NRSRO corporate governance, organization, and management of conflicts of interest. Requires the SEC to issue specified rules to prohibit, or require the management and disclosure of, conflicts of interest relating to the issuance of credit ratings by an NRSRO. Requires each NRSRO to establish policies and procedures to ensure a look-back review to determine whether a conflict of interest exists in any case in which an employee of a person subject to a credit rating of an NRSRO, or of the issuer, underwriter, or sponsor of a security or money market instrument subject to a credit rating of the NRSRO, was employed by the NRSRO and participated in determining credit ratings for the person or the securities or money market instruments during the one-year period preceding the date an action was taken with respect to the credit rating. Requires the SEC to: (1) conduct periodic reviews of NRSRO compliance with this look-back requirement; (2) establish an office that administers SEC rules governing NRSRO practices; (3) require each NRSRO to disclose publicly information on initial ratings and subsequent changes to them; and (4) prescribe rules requiring each NRSRO to adopt certain credit ratings methodologies and an internal control system, establish policies and procedures designed to assess the risk that investors may not receive payment in accordance with the terms of securities and money market instruments they invest in, and define clearly and apply consistently any credit rating symbol used by that NRSRO. Requires an NRSRO to report to the SEC any case where it can reasonably be expected to know that a person associated with the NRSRO within the previous five years obtained employment with any issuer, underwriter, or sponsor of an instrument for which the NRSRO had issued a credit rating during the 12-month period before such employment. Directs the SEC to require NRSROs to publish with each credit rating a form disclosing information about the assumptions underlying the procedures and methodologies used to determine the credit rating. Requires each NRSRO to designate a compliance officer to review and ensure NRSRO compliance with federal requirements. Prohibits an NRSRO that provides a credit rating to an issuer, underwriter, or placement agent of a security from providing non-rating services to such person in determining a credit rating, including: (1) risk management advisory services; and (2) consulting services regarding any merger, sales, or disposition of the assets of an issuer.

Section 6003

Declares that in private actions against an NRSRO it shall be sufficient for pleading any required state of mind that the complaint state with particularity facts giving rise to a strong inference that the NRSRO was grossly negligent in violating the securities laws. Grants any purchaser of a security given a rating by an NRSRO the right to recover for damages if the process of determining the credit rating was grossly negligent and a substantial factor in the economic loss the investor suffered. Sets the statute of limitations on such an action at two years after discovery of the facts constituting the violation and three years after the initial issuance of the rating.

Section 6004

Directs the SEC to require issuers to disclose preliminary credit ratings received from NRSROs on structured products and corporate debt.

Section 6007

Requires the SEC to revise Regulation FD (general rule regarding selective disclosure by an issuer of material nonpublic information regarding that issuer or its securities) to remove the exemption from it for NRSROs and other credit rating agencies.

Section 6008

Instructs the SEC to establish the Credit Ratings Agency Advisory Board.

Section 6009

Amends the FDIA, the Federal Housing Enterprises Financial Safety and Soundness Act of 1992, the Investment Company Act of 1940, the Revised Statutes, and the Securities Exchange Act of 1934 to remove references to credit ratings to reflect the provisions of this Act.

Section 6010

Requires specified federal agencies to: (1) review any of their regulations that require the use of an assessment of the credit-worthiness of a security or money market instrument; and (2) remove any requirement of reliance on credit ratings and substitute a standard of credit-worthiness deemed appropriate by the agency. Directs the Comptroller General to report to Congress on the use of credit ratings by federal agencies and recommendations for legislation or rulemaking to reduce agency reliance on such ratings.

Section 6011

Directs the SEC to revise the Code of Federal Regulations to require that the random sample of ratings histories of credit ratings required under its rules to be disclosed on the website of an NRSRO also be provided to the SEC in a format consistent with publication on the EDGAR system.

Section 6012

Declares without force or effect Rule 436(g) promulgated by the SEC under the Securities Act of 1933. (Rule 436(g) exempts credit ratings provided by NRSROs from being considered a part of the registration statement prepared or certified by a person under such Act.)

Section 6013

Directs the Comptroller General to study and report to Congress on the implementation of this subtitle, including: (1) the appropriateness of relying on ratings for use in federal, state, and local securities and banking regulations, as well as for determining capital requirements; (2) the effect of liability in private actions arising under the Securities Exchange Act of 1934; (3) alternative means for compensating credit rating agencies that would create incentives for accurate credit ratings and what, if any, statutory changes would be required to permit or facilitate the use of such alternative means of compensation; and (4) alternative methodologies to assess credit risk, including market-based measures. Directs the SEC to study and report to

Congress on: (1) a system that assigns NRSROs on a rotating basis to issuers seeking a credit rating; (2) the effect of new requirements on NRSRO registration; (3) credit ratings of different classes of bonds; (4) meaningful multidigit ratings system; and (5) ratings standardization.

Subtitle C - Investor Protection Act

Investor Protection Act of 2009 -

Part 1 - Disclosure

Section 7101

Amends the Securities Exchange Act of 1934 to establish the Investor Advisory Committee to advise and consult with SEC on: (1) regulatory priorities and issues regarding new products, trading strategies, fee structures, and the effectiveness of disclosures; (2) initiatives to protect investor interest; and (3) initiatives to promote investor confidence in the integrity of the marketplace.

Section 7102

Amends the Securities Act of 1933, the Securities Exchange Act of 1934, the Investment Advisers Act of 1940 and Investment Company Act of 1940 to authorize the SEC to gather information, communicate with investors or other members of the public, and engage in temporary or experimental programs in the public interest or for protection of investors.

Section 7103

Amends the Securities Exchange Act of 1934 and the Investment Advisers Act of 1940 to direct the SEC to establish a standard of conduct (fiduciary duty) for brokers, dealers, and investment advisers, without regard to their financial or other interests, to act in the best interest of the customer when providing personalized investment advice about securities to a retail customer.

Section 7104

Requires the SEC to publish a study that examines the nature of "retail customers" and the range of products and services sold to them, as well as the sellers or providers, and related information such customers should receive before their purchase of investment products or services. Authorizes the SEC, following completion of such study, to promulgate rules requiring that the appropriate persons or entities provide designated documents or information to retail customers prior to the purchase of identified investment products or services.

Section 7105

Amends the Securities Exchange Act of 1934 to revise SEC requirements for beneficial ownership and short-swing profit reporting.

Section 7106

Amends the Investment Company Act of 1940 to prescribe recordkeeping requirements for each person with custody or use of a registered investment company's securities, deposits, or credits.

Section 7107

Directs the SEC to study and report to Congress on the need for enhanced examination and enforcement resources for investment advisers.

Section 7108

Directs the Comptroller General to study and report to Congress on the regulation and oversight of financial planning.

Part 2 - Enforcement and Remedies

Section 7201

Amends the Securities Exchange Act of 1934 and the Investment Advisers Act of 1940 to authorize the SEC to restrict or prohibit mandatory pre-dispute arbitration affecting customers or clients of brokers and dealers, including municipal securities dealers.

Section 7202

Directs the Comptroller General to study and report to Congress on: (1) the costs to the parties of an arbitration proceeding using the arbitration system operated by the Financial Industry Regulatory Authority and overseen by the

SEC as compared to litigation; and (2) the percentage of recovery of the total amount of a claim in an arbitration proceeding and overseen by the SEC.

Section 7203

Amends the Securities Exchange Act of 1934 to set forth monetary incentives and protection for whistleblowers, including up to 30% of the monetary sanctions imposed in an action that results in monetary sanctions exceeding $1 million if the whistleblowers voluntarily provided original information to the SEC that led to the successful enforcement of the action. Establishes the Securities and Exchange Commission Investor Protection Fund to: (1) pay awards to whistleblowers; and (2) fund investor education initiatives to help investors protect themselves against securities fraud or other violations of securities laws and regulations. Prohibits acts of retaliation against an employee, contractor, or agent for providing information to the SEC.

Section 7206

Amends the Securities Exchange Act of 1934 with respect to the registration and regulation of brokers, dealers, municipal securities dealers, and transfer agents, and the Investment Advisers Act of 1940 with respect to registration of investment advisers, to revise requirements for collateral bars or suspensions in the case of persons associated, or seeking to be associated, with any of them who is subject to penalties for specified offenses.

Section 7207

Amends the Securities Act of 1933, the Investment Company Act of 1940, and the Investment Advisers Act of 1940 to subject to liability for prosecution and penalties persons who aid and abet violations of such Acts.

Section 7209

Expands SEC enforcement and remedies, including: (1) deadlines and procedures for completing compliance examinations, inspections, and enforcement actions for violations of securities laws; (2) nationwide service of subpoenas; (3) imposition of civil penalties in cease and desist proceedings; (4) enforcement authority over any person who at the time of the alleged misconduct was a member or employee of specified bodies (formerly associated persons); (5) the sharing of privileged information with other authorities; (5) increased access to grand jury information; (6) recklessness as an element of the aiding and abetting standard of knowledge; and (7) SEC extraterritorial jurisdiction with respect to antifraud activities.

Section 7217

Amends the Investment Company Act of 1940 to revise requirements for the fidelity bonding of registered management companies.

Section 7218

Amends the Securities Exchange Act of 1934 and the Investment Company Act of 1940 to subject to reasonable periodic, special, or other information and document requests by SEC representatives conducting surveillance or risk assessments all securities markets, national securities exchanges, their members, brokers or dealers who transact a business in securities through the medium of any such member, SEC-registered securities associations, -registered brokers or dealers, -registered municipal securities dealers, -registered securities information processors, -registered transfer agents, NRSROs, -registered clearing agencies, and the Municipal Securities Rulemaking Board.

Section 7219

Amends the Investment Company Act of 1940 to revise the record-examination requirements for registered investment companies, and each underwriter, broker, dealer, or investment adviser that is a majority-owned subsidiary of such a company.

Section 7220

Amends the Securities Exchange Act of 1934 to make any person who controls a person liable under such Act also jointly and severally liable to the SEC in certain actions it may bring.

Section 7221

Applies anti-fraud provisions to any security that is not a government security.

Section 7222

Extends SEC rulemaking authority to the prescription of rules on proxy access.

Part 3 - Commission Funding and Organization

Section 7301

Authorizes appropriations for the SEC for FY2010-FY2015.

Section 7302

Amends the Investment Advisers Act of 1940 to direct the SEC to promulgate rules to collect fees annually from investment advisers to recover the cost of inspections and examinations of registered investment advisers.

Section 7303

Amends the Securities Exchange Act of 1934 to revise requirements for: (1) payment of transaction fees and assessments; and (2) mid-year adjustments to such fees and assessments to recapture projection windfalls for further rate reductions.

Section 7304

Requires the SEC to hire an independent consultant to examine and report to the SEC and Congress on SEC internal operations, structure, funding, and the need for comprehensive reform, including the SEC's relationship with and reliance upon self-regulatory organizations and other entities under SEC oversight relevant to the regulation of securities and the protection of investors.

Section 7305

Establishes within the SEC the Capital Markets Safety Board to investigate failed institutions and report to the SEC on what caused them to fail.

Section 7306

Requires the SEC to report to certain congressional committees on the implementation of reforms in the wake of the discovery of fraud by Bernie Madoff.

Section 7307

Authorizes the SEC and the CFTC to form and operate a joint advisory committee to identify emerging issues and regulatory risks, assess their implications for market participants, and recommend solutions.

Part 4 - Additional Commission Reforms

Section 7401

Amends the Securities Exchange Act of 1934 regarding manipulative and deceptive devices to: (1) make it unlawful for any person to effect, accept, or facilitate a transaction involving the loan or borrowing of securities in contravention of SEC rules and regulations; (2) revise requirements for the reporting of lost and stolen securities to include canceled securities or any other category the SEC may prescribe; (3) require fingerprinting of partners, directors, officers, and employees of registered securities information processors, national securities exchanges, and national securities associations; and (4) declare void any condition, stipulation, or provision binding any person to waive compliance with the rules of a self-regulatory organization.

Section 7407

Directs the SEC, the Public Company Accounting Oversight Board (PCAOB), and a designated standard setting body to provide oral testimony annually for five years to the Committee on Financial Services of the House of Representatives regarding efforts to reduce the complexity in financial reporting in order to provide more accurate and clear financial information to investors.

Section 7408

Revises the prohibition against unlawful credit extension (margin lending) to customers.

Section 7409

Revises the Securities Exchange Act of 1934 and the Investment Company Act of 1940 to extend SEC authority to limit disclosure of information to information relating to an examination, surveillance, or risk assessment of a person, and to any information supplied by a self-regulatory organization. Declares that nothing shall prevent the SEC from complying with a request for information from the PCAOB.

Section 7411

Revises the composition of the Municipal Securities Rulemaking Board, as well as Board nomination and election procedures.

Section 7412

Amends the Investment Company Act of 1940 to extend the definition of "interested person" to any natural person who is a member of a class of persons the SEC determines are unlikely to exercise an appropriate degree of independence due to: (1) a material business or professional relationship with such company or any affiliated person of such company; or (2) a close familial relationship with any natural person who is an affiliated person of such company. Repeals two current requirements dealing with execution of portfolio transactions and the lending of money or other property.

Section 7413

Amends the Investment Company Act of 1940 to authorize the SEC to limit the extent to which a registered open-end investment company may own, hold, or invest in illiquid securities or other illiquid property.

Section 7414

Directs the Comptroller General to study and report to Congress on SEC employees who leave the agency to work for financial institutions regulated by the SEC.

Section 7415

Directs the Comptroller General to evaluate and report to Congress on the costs and benefits of compliance with the Sarbanes-Oxley Act of 2002 requirements for assessment of internal controls by the management of issuers who are neither accelerated filers nor large accelerated filers.

Section 7416

Directs the SEC to study and report to specified congressional committees on the inclusion of revenue as a criteria used in defining a smaller reporting company to account for smaller public companies with public floats less than $700 million and revenues less than $250 million.

Section 7417

Establishes a Financial Reporting Forum composed of certain senior federal agency personnel to report annually to Congress on immediate and long-term issues critical to financial reporting.

Section 7418

Amends the Investment Advisers Act of 1940 to subject to domiciliary state registration requirements certain mid-sized investment advisers otherwise not exempt from federal registration requirements.

Section 7419

Directs the SEC to adopt a rule making it unlawful for an SEC-registered investment adviser to have custody of funds or securities of a client the value of which exceeds $10 million, unless: (1) the funds and securities are maintained with a qualified custodian either in a separate account for each client under the client's name, or in accounts that contain only client funds and securities under the name of the investment adviser as agent or trustee for the client; and (2) the qualified custodian does not directly or indirectly provide investment advice with respect to such funds or securities.

Section 7420

Requires the SEC to: (1) appoint an Ombudsman to act as a liaison between the SEC and any affected person who may have a problem dealing with the SEC as a result of its regulatory activities; and (2) revise its regulations to require due diligence on the part of brokers and dealers and other specified paying agents to search for lost securityholders who have been sent checks for dividends, interest, and other valuable property which have not yet been negotiated.

Section 7422

Requires every institutional investment manager that effects a short sale of an equity security to file daily with the SEC specified short sale disclosures. Makes it unlawful to effect manipulative short sales of securities. Requires registered brokers or dealers to notify customers that: (1) they may elect not to allow their fully paid securities to be used in connection with short sales; and (2) the broker or dealer may receive compensation in connection with lending the customer's securities.

Section 7423

Revises requirements for SEC filing procedures with respect to proposed rule changes.

Part 5 - Securities Investor Protection Act Amendments

Section 7501

Amends the Securities Investor Protection Act of 1970 (SIPA) to increase: (1) the minimum assessment paid by Securities Investor Protection Corporation (SIPC) members; (2) the borrowing limit on Treasury loans; (3) the standard maximum cash advance for each customer (including an inflation adjustment); and (4) the fine for certain prohibited acts, including misrepresentation of SIPC membership or protection.

Section 7504

Amends SIPA with respect to: (1) SIPC trusteeship in liquidation proceedings; (2) insider ineligibility for SIPC advances; and (3) futures held in a portfolio margin securities account.

Section 7506

Revises requirements for determining whether an SIPC member qualifies for SIPC use of the direct payment procedure to satisfy customer claims without a liquidation proceeding. Increases from $250,000 to $850,000 the maximum aggregate amount of claims of all customers of a SIPC member that, among other criteria, shall allow the SIPC to use the direct payment procedure.

Section 7510

Directs the Comptroller General to study and report to Congress whether SIPC should be required to impose risk-based assessments, on member brokers and dealers, based on risk in order to maintain the SIPC Fund adequately and to provide additional levels of coverage on an optional basis.

Part 6 - Sarbanes-Oxley Act Amendments

Section 7601

Amends the Sarbanes-Oxley Act of 2002 to include brokers and dealers within its purview. Authorizes the PCAOB to conduct and require a program of inspection of registered public accounting firms that provide audit reports for brokers and dealers. Prescribes a scheme for allocating accounting support fees among brokers and dealers. Refers to the appropriate self-regulatory organization any investigations concerning an audit report for a broker or dealer that is subject to the organization's jurisdiction.

Section 7602

Authorizes the PCAOB to provide to a foreign auditor oversight authority all information relating to a public accounting firm within the foreign oversight authority's jurisdiction.

Section 7603

Revises requirements for the production of audit work papers by a foreign public accounting firm or a registered public accounting firm that relies upon the work of the foreign firm. Requires a foreign public accounting firm to produce its audit work papers and all other documents to the SEC or the PCAOB upon request if the firm issues an audit report, performs audit work, or conducts interim reviews upon which a registered public accounting firm relies in the conduct of an audit or interim review. (Continues to require a registered public accounting firm relying upon the work of a foreign public accounting firm to produce the foreign firm's work papers upon SEC or PCAOB request.)

Section 7605

Modifies the procedure under which civil penalties obtained by the SEC shall be added to and become part of a disgorgement fund established for the relief of victims of the violation. Requires the amount of any settlement of a judicial or administrative action to be added to the disgorgement fund.

Section 7606

Exempts smaller securities issuers that are not accelerated filers from the requirement that a registered public accounting firm that prepares or issues the issuer's audit report attest to, and report on, the assessment made by the issuer's management. Directs the SEC to study and report to Congress on how it could reduce the burden for certain companies (whose market capitalization is between $75 million and $250 million for the relevant reporting period) of complying with such requirement while maintaining investor protections for such companies.

Section 7607

Modifies federal criminal law granting whistleblower protections for employees of publicly traded companies to prohibit subsidiaries and affiliates of an issuer from engaging in specified acts of discrimination or retaliation.

Section 7608

Declares that nothing shall prevent the PCAOB from responding to requests from specified congressional committees for reports about PCAOB activities or programs, provided that any confidential information shall be subject to certain nondisclosure requirements.

Section 7609

Requires the PCAOB to appoint an ombudsman that shall act as a liaison between the Board and: (1) any registered public accounting firm or issuer concerning issues or disputes of any audit report with respect to that issuer; and (2) any affected registered public accounting firm or issuer regarding regulatory activities of the PCAOB, and issues caused by the relationships of registered public accounting firms and issuers generally.

Section 7610

Redesignates the PCAOB as the Auditing Oversight Board.

Part 7 - Senior Investment Protection

Section 7703

Directs the SEC to establish a program of grants to states to: (1) investigate and prosecute misleading and fraudulent marketing practices, or (2) develop educational materials and training to reduce misleading and fraudulent marketing of financial products toward seniors.

Section 7706

Authorizes appropriations for FY2011-FY2015.

Part 8 - Registration of Municipal Financial Advisors

Section 7801

Amends the Securities Exchange Act of 1934 to require municipal financial advisers to register with the SEC.

TITLE VI - FEDERAL INSURANCE OFFICE

Federal Insurance Office Act of 2009 -

Section 8002

Establishes in the Treasury the Federal Insurance Office (FIO) to: (1) monitor the insurance industry; (2) identify issues or gaps in the regulation of insurers that could contribute to a systemic crisis in the insurance industry or the U.S. financial system; (3) monitor the extent to which traditionally underserved communities and consumers, minorities, and low- and moderate-income persons have access to affordable insurance products covering all lines of insurance, except health insurance; (4) recommend to the Financial Services Oversight Council that it designate an insurer as one subject to stricter standards; (5) assist in administering the Terrorism Insurance Program; and (6) advise on major domestic and prudential international insurance policy issues. Extends the authority of the Office to all lines of insurance except health insurance. Sets forth a limited preemption of state insurance measures. Authorizes appropriations for the FIO. Authorizes the Secretary and the United States Trade Representative (USTR), jointly, on behalf of the United States, to negotiate and enter into bilateral or multilateral recognition agreements with foreign governments, authorities, or regulatory entities that provide for recognition of prudential measures with respect to the business of insurance or reinsurance that achieve a level of protection for consumers substantially equivalent to the level of protection achieved under state insurance or reinsurance regulation.

Section 8003

Requires the FIO Director to study and report to specified congressional committees on: (1) the global reinsurance market; and (2) modernization and improvement of insurance regulation in the United States.

Section 8005

Expresses the sense of Congress that mortgage lenders should provide loan applicants with a simplified loan contract summary, including an easy-to-read list of basic loan terms, payment information, the existence of prepayment penalties or balloon payments, and escrow information.

TITLE VII - MORTGAGE REFORM AND ANTI-PREDATORY LENDING ACT

Mortgage Reform and Anti-Predatory Lending Act -

Subtitle A - Residential Mortgage Loan Origination Standards

Section 9002

Amends the Truth in Lending Act (TILA) to prescribe fiduciary standards for originators of residential mortgages, including complete and timely written disclosure of: (1) the comparative costs and benefits of each residential mortgage loan product presented by the originator; (2) the nature of the originator's relationship to the consumer, including the cost of services provided by the originator; and (3) any relevant conflicts of interest between originator and consumer.

Section 9003

Prohibits steering incentives in connection with mortgage loan origination. Directs the federal banking agencies to prescribe proscriptions against specified mortgage origination practices, including steering any consumer to a residential mortgage loan that: (1) the consumer lacks a reasonable ability to repay; (2) does not provide a consumer refinancing a residential mortgage loan with a net tangible benefit; or (3) has predatory characteristics or effects (such as equity stripping, excessive fees, or abusive terms).

Section 9004

Sets forth the maximum liability of a mortgage originator to a consumer for violation of the residential mortgage loan origination requirements of this title, in addition to court costs and attorney fees, at the greater of: (1) actual damages; or (2) three times the total amount of direct and indirect compensation or gain accruing to the originator in connection with the loan involved.

Section 9005

Requires the federal banking agencies jointly to prohibit or condition terms, acts, or practices relating to residential mortgage loans found to be abusive, unfair, deceptive, predatory, inconsistent with reasonable underwriting standards.

Section 9006

Requires the Secretary of Housing and Urban Development (HUD) to study and report to Congress on regulatory requirements that would provide: (1) widespread use of shared appreciation mortgages to strengthen local housing markets; (2) new opportunities for affordable homeownership; and (3) homeowners at risk of foreclosure with the ability to refinance or modify their mortgages.

Subtitle B - Minimum Standards for Mortgages

Section 9101

Prescribes minimum standards for residential mortgage loans, including a requirement that a residential mortgage loan creditor: (1) make a reasonable and good faith determination based upon verified and documented information that the consumer has a reasonable ability to repay the loan and its applicable taxes, insurance, and assessments; and (2) use a fully amortizing repayment schedule for purposes of determining a consumer's ability to repay a variable rate loan that defers repayment of principal or interest. Denies application of such standards to reverse mortgages.

Section 9102

Prohibits a creditor from extending credit in connection with any residential mortgage loan that involves a refinancing of a prior existing residential mortgage loan unless the creditor reasonably and in good faith determines, at the time the loan is consummated and on the basis of information known by or obtained in good faith by the creditor, that the refinanced loan will provide a net tangible benefit to the consumer.

Section 9103

Authorizes any creditor with respect to any qualified residential mortgage loan (including any assignee or securitizer of such loan, as well as any FHA-insured reverse mortgage) which meets specified requirements, to presume that the loan has met the minimum standards of this subtitle. Requires publication of average prime offer rates and APR thresholds.

Section 9104

Permits civil actions for rescission of a residential mortgage loan if a creditor has committed specified abuses. Limits the liability of good faith assignees or securitizers of a residential mortgage loan to loan rescission and to certain obligor costs. Allows such an assignee or securitizer to avoid liability if it provides a satisfactory cure within 90 days after notice of the violation from the consumer. Shields assignees and securitizers from class action suits for certain violations.

Section 9105

Permits a consumer who has the right to mortgage loan rescission to assert such right as a defense to foreclosure.

Section 9106

Prohibits specified practices, including: (1) certain prepayment penalties; (2) single premium credit insurance; (3) mandatory arbitration or other nonjudicial procedure (except for reverse mortgages); (4) residential mortgage loan terms that waive a statutory cause of action by the consumer; and (5) mortgages with negative amortization (except, again, for reverse mortgages), unless certain disclosures are made and a first-time borrower receives homeownership counseling. Requires a creditor or mortgage originator, before loan consummation or loan refinancing, to disclose the protection provided by a state anti-deficiency law and its significance for the consumer upon the loss of that protection. (A state anti-deficiency law shields a consumer mortgagor from liability for any deficiency between a foreclosure sale price and the outstanding balance of the mortgage.) Requires a residential mortgage loan creditor to disclose before settlement: (1) the creditor's policy regarding partial payments and their application to the mortgage; and (2) whether partial payments will be placed in escrow.

Section 9110

Doubles civil money penalties for certain violations.

Section 9111

Shields a creditor, assignee, or securitizer from liability and rescission in the case of borrower fraud or deception.

Section 9112

Requires a six-month notice period before a hybrid adjustable rate mortgage is reset.

Section 9113

Prescribes creditor disclosures for: (1) variable rate residential mortgage loans for which an escrow or impound account will be established to pay taxes, insurance, and assessments; and (2) periodic statements for residential mortgage loans.

Section 9115

Directs the HUD Secretary to establish a grants program to enable low- and moderate-income homeowners and tenants to obtain legal assistance associated with foreclosure. Authorizes appropriations for FY2009-FY2012.

Section 9117

Directs the Comptroller General to study and report to Congress on the effects that enactment of this Act will have upon the availability and affordability of credit for consumers, small businesses, homebuyers, and mortgage lending, including the effect upon: (1) the mortgage market for mortgages that are not within the safe harbor provided in this Act; (2) the ability of prospective homebuyers to obtain financing; and (3) the refinance ability of homeowners facing resets or adjustments.

Section 9118

Authorizes state attorneys general to bring an action to enforce the requirements of subtitle A (residential mortgage loan origination) and subtitle B (minimum standards for residential mortgage loans).

Subtitle C - High-Cost Mortgages

Section 9201

Prescribes standards for points and fees related to: (1) high-cost mortgages; (2) open-end consumer credit plans; and (3) bona fide discount points and prepayment penalties.

Section 9202

Repeals the allowance of prepayment penalties for certain mortgages. Prohibits a high-cost mortgage from containing a scheduled payment that is more than twice as large (balloon payment) as the average of earlier scheduled payments.

Section 9203

Prescribes additional requirements for certain mortgages. Prohibits a creditor from: (1) recommending default on an existing debt prior to and in connection with the closing of a high-cost mortgage that refinances any portion of such debt; (2) imposing late payment fees in connection with a high-cost mortgage except in compliance with specified requirements; (3) accelerating debt on a high-cost mortgage (except in certain circumstances); or (4) financing, in connection with any high-cost mortgage, either a prepayment fee or penalty payable by the consumer if the creditor is the noteholder of the note being refinanced. Prohibits the creditor of a high-cost mortgage from implementing certain evasions, structured transactions, and reciprocal arrangements. Prohibits a creditor from charging a consumer any fee to modify, renew, extend, or amend a high-cost mortgage, or to defer any payment due under such mortgage, unless the modification, renewal, extension, or amendment results in a lower APR on the mortgage for the consumer, and the fee is comparable to fees imposed for similar consumer credit transactions secured by a consumer's principal dwelling. Prohibits any fee for payoff statements, except a processing fee. Requires a creditor, as a prerequisite to extending consumer credit under a high-cost mortgage, to receive certification from a HUD-approved counselor that the consumer has received counseling on the advisability of the mortgage. Prohibits any creditor from knowingly or intentionally engaging in the unfair act or practice of flipping in connection with a high-cost mortgage. Defines flipping as the making of a loan or extension of credit in the form a high-cost mortgage to a consumer which refinances an existing mortgage when the new loan or extension of credit does not have reasonable, net tangible benefit to the consumer considering all of the circumstances. Prescribes a procedure by which a high cost loan creditor or assignee that, acting in good faith, commits an unintentional violation of these prohibitions and other requirements may make timely corrections and avoid liability for the violation.

Subtitle D - Office of Housing Counseling

Expand and Preserve Home Ownership Through Counseling Act -

Section 9302

Amends the Department of Housing and Urban Development Act to establish within HUD the Office of Housing Counseling, whose Director shall have primary responsibility for all activities and matters relating to both homeownership and rental housing counseling.

Section 9303

Amends the Housing and Urban Development Act of 1968 to require the HUD Secretary to: (1) prescribe counseling procedures for homeownership and rental counseling; and (2) provide for certification of computer software programs for consumers to evaluate different residential mortgage loan proposals. Requires the Director to: (1) develop and conduct national public service multimedia campaigns promoting housing counseling; and (2) use specified funds to conduct foreclosure rescue education programs, with emphasis upon retirement and low-income minority communities. Authorizes appropriations for FY2009-FY2011.

Section 9304

Requires the HUD Secretary to provide financial assistance (grants) to HUD-approved housing counseling agencies and state housing finance agencies that offer homeownership and rental counseling. Authorizes appropriations for FY2009-FY2012 for: (1) the Office of Housing Counseling; (2) the Director of Housing Counseling; and (3) assistance to entities providing homeownership and rental counseling.

Section 9305

Requires an organization that receives federal assistance for counseling activities to be HUD-certified.

Section 9306

Directs the HUD Secretary to study and report to Congress on: (1) the root causes of home loan defaults and foreclosures, including the role of escrow accounts in helping prime and nonprime borrowers to avoid defaults and foreclosures; and (2) the role of computer registries of mortgages, including those used for trading mortgage loans.

Section 9307

Directs the HUD Secretary to establish on a census tract basis a default and foreclosure database on mortgage loans for one- to four-unit residential properties, and to make such information publicly available.

Section 9309

Directs the Secretary to develop a funds-tracking system, including accountability and transparency criteria, to ensure that grant recipients use all amounts of financial assistance in accordance with specified requirements.

Section 9310

Amends the Real Estate Settlement Procedures Act of 1974 (RESPA) to require the Director of the Consumer Financial Protection Agency to: (1) prepare, at least once every five years, a booklet to help federally related mortgage loan applicants of different ethnic and cultural backgrounds to understand the nature and costs of real estate settlement services; and (2) distribute to all lenders that make federally related mortgage loans both the booklets and lists of HUD-certified homeownership counselors.

Section 9311

Requires the HUD Secretary to inform potential homebuyers of the availability and importance of obtaining an independent home inspection.

Section 9312

Allocates specified funds to the Neighborhood Reinvestment Corporation for activities to make borrowers who are delinquent on certain loans aware of the dangers of fraudulent activities associated with foreclosure.

Subtitle E - Mortgage Servicing

Section 9401

Amends TILA to require a creditor in a non-credit card consumer credit transaction secured by a first lien on the principal dwelling (other than a reverse mortgage) to establish an escrow or impound account for mandatory periodic payments or premiums (including taxes, insurance, and ground rents). Prohibits making an escrow or impound account a condition of a real property sale contract or a loan secured by a first deed of trust or mortgage on the consumer's principal dwelling unless specified circumstances exist. Requires such escrow or impound account to remain in existence for at least five years until sufficient equity exists so that private mortgage insurance is no longer required, or unless the underlying mortgage is terminated. States that: (1) escrow accounts need not be established for loans secured by shares in a cooperative; and (2) insurance premiums need not be included in escrow accounts for loans secured by condominium units if the condominium association has an obligation to unit owners to maintain a master insurance policy. Requires: (1) escrow accounts to be established in a federally insured depository institution; and (2) each creditor to pay interest on the amount held in such accounts as required by state or federal law. Requires specified consumer disclosures regarding a mandatory escrow or impound account before consummation of the credit transaction giving rise to such account.

Section 9402

Requires creditors to provide specified disclosures for consumers who waive escrow services.

Section 9403

Amends RESPA to prohibit the servicer of a federally related mortgage from engaging in certain practices, including obtaining force-placed hazard insurance unless there is reason to believe the borrower has failed to comply with the loan contract requirements. (Force-placed hazard insurance is coverage obtained by the servicer when the borrower has failed to comply with hazard insurance requirements under the terms of the mortgage.) Prescribes notice and borrower non-response requirements for loan servicers to obtain force-placed insurance. Doubles the penalties for loan servicer noncompliance with RESPA disclosure requirements. Reduces from 20 days to five days the time limit within which loan servicers are required to respond to borrower inquiries. Requires any remaining escrow balance that is within the control of the loan servicer at the time the loan is paid off to be: (1) promptly returned to the borrower within 20 business days; or (2) credited to a similar account for a new mortgage loan to the borrower with the same lender.

Section 9404

Amends TILA to prohibit a loan servicer, except in a specified circumstance, from failing to credit a payment to the consumer's account as of the date of receipt. Requires a creditor or servicer of a home loan to send an accurate payoff balance no later than seven business days after receipt of a written request for it.

Section 9405

Requires repayment disclosures regarding a first mortgage- or lien-secured consumer credit transaction to take into account the amount of monthly escrow payments, including: (1) the taxable assessed value of the real property securing the transaction after consummation of the transaction; (2) the value of any improvements on the property or to be constructed on it; and (3) the replacement costs of the property for hazard insurance in the initial year after the transaction.

Subtitle F - Appraisal Activities

Section 9501

Amends TILA to set forth property appraisal requirements for a creditor who extends subprime mortgage credit to a consumer, including: (1) a written appraisal performed by a qualified appraiser who conducts a physical property visit of the interior of the mortgaged property; (2) a free copy of such appraisal to the applicant before the transaction closing date; and (3) a statement by the creditor at the time of the initial mortgage application that the appraisal is for its sole use, and that the applicant, at its own expense, may choose to have a separate appraisal. Requires a creditor to obtain a second appraisal from a different qualified appraiser if the purpose of a subprime mortgage (other than a HUD-insured reverse mortgage) is to finance the purchase or acquisition of the mortgaged property from a person within 180 days of the purchase or acquisition of such property by that person at a price lower than the current sale price of the property.

Section 9502

Declares unfair and deceptive certain practices relating to consumer credit transaction secured by the consumer's principal dwelling. Includes among unfair and deceptive practices any appraisal of a property offered as security in which a person with an interest in the underlying transaction compensates, coerces, extorts, colludes, instructs, induces, bribes, or intimidates a person conducting or involved in the appraisal. Includes, in addition, among such practices: (1) mischaracterizing, or suborning mischaracterization of the appraised value of the property securing the extension of the credit; (2) seeking to influence an appraiser or otherwise to encourage a targeted value in order to facilitate the transaction; and (3) withholding or threatening to withhold timely payment for an appraisal report or for appraisal services rendered. Prohibits any certified or licensed appraiser or appraisal management company from having an interest, financial or otherwise, in the property or transaction involving the appraisal. Requires designated federal agencies to prescribe implementing regulations jointly. Subjects unfair and deceptive practices to civil penalties.

Section 9503

Amends the Financial Institutions Reform, Recovery, and Enforcement Act of 1989 (FIRREA) to provide the Appraisal Subcommittee of the Federal Financial Institutions Examination Council (FIEC) with a consumer protection mandate. Directs the Subcommittee to monitor the efforts of, and requirements established by, states and federal financial institutions regulatory agencies to protect consumers from improper appraisal practices and from predations of unlicensed appraisers in consumer credit transactions secured by a consumer's principal dwelling. Requires the Subcommittee to detail in its annual report to Congress: (1) the results of all audits of state appraiser regulatory agencies; and (2) an accounting of disapproved actions and warnings taken in the previous year, including the conditions causing the disapproval and the actions taken to achieve compliance. Requires meetings of the Subcommittee to be open to the public. Requires: (1) all property appraisals performed within a state to be prepared by appraisers licensed or certified within the state where the property is located; and (2) all appraisal reviews to be performed by an appraiser licensed or certified by a state appraisal board. Requires the Subcommittee to monitor state requirements for the registration and supervision of an appraisal management company. Directs the Subcommittee to maintain a national registry of appraisal management companies that either are: (1) registered with and subject to supervision of a state appraiser certifying and licensing agency; or (2) operating subsidiaries of a federally regulated financial institution. Requires the Appraiser Qualifications Board of the Appraisal Foundation to establish minimum qualifications a state must apply in the registration of appraisal management companies, including specified requirements. Requires the appropriate federal financial institution regulatory agency to develop regulations affecting the operations of any appraisal management company that is a subsidiary owned and controlled by a federally regulated financial institution. Sets forth: (1) registration limitations; (2) additional state agency reporting requirements; and (3) revised registry fees. Authorizes the Subcommittee to award grants to state appraiser certifying and licensing agencies in order to support their compliance with this Act. Authorizes the Subcommittee to: (1) remove a state licensed or certified appraiser or a registered appraisal management company from a national registry on an interim basis pending state agency action on licensing, certification, registration, and disciplinary proceedings; (2) impose sanctions against a state agency that fails to have an effective appraiser regulatory program; and (3) impose interim actions and suspensions against a state agency as an alternative to, or in advance of, derecognition of a state agency. Requires a state appraiser certifying or licensing agency to issue a reciprocal certification or license for an individual with a valid certification or license from another state in compliance with this Act whose licensure standards meet or exceed those of the first state. Requires the Subcommittee to monitor each state appraiser certifying and licensing agency to determine whether: (1) its policies, practices, and procedures are consistent with the purposes of maintaining appraiser independence; and (2) such state maintains effective regulations, and policies regarding maintaining appraiser independence. Requires the Subcommittee, one year after enactment of this Act, to establish and operate an Appraisal Complaint National Hotline, including a toll-free telephone number and an email address, if none exists by that time. Directs the Subcommittee to promulgate regulations to implement quality control standards governing automated valuation models (computerized models used by mortgage originators and secondary market issuers to determine the collateral worth of a mortgage secured by a consumer's principal dwelling). Prohibits broker price opinions from being used as the primary basis to evaluate property for loan origination in connection with a residential mortgage loan secured by such property. Amends the Federal Financial Institutions Examination Council Act of 1978 to require that at all times at least one member of the Appraisal Subcommittee have demonstrated knowledge and competence through licensure, certification, or professional designation within the appraisal profession.

Section 9504

Directs the Comptroller General to study and report to Congress on possible improvements in the appraisal process generally, and specifically on the consistency in and the effectiveness of, and possible improvements in, state compliance efforts and programs.

Section 9505

Amends the Equal Credit Opportunity Act (ECOA) to revise requirements that creditors provide loan applicants a copy of the appraisal report used in connection with the applicant's application for a loan that is or would have been secured by a lien on residential real property. Repeals the condition that the loan applicant request the copy. Requires a creditor to furnish the applicant a copy of all written appraisals and valuations within three days after the closing of the loan.

Section 9506

Amends RESPA to require the standard real estate settlement form to disclose, in the case of an appraisal coordinated by an appraisal management company, the fee paid directly by the company to the appraiser as well as the company's administration fee.

Subtitle G - Sense of Congress Regarding the Importance of Government Sponsored Enterprises Reform

Section 9601

Expresses the sense of Congress that efforts to enhance the terms of residential mortgage credit and practices would be incomplete without enactment of meaningful structural reforms of the Federal National Mortgage Association (Fannie Mae) and the Federal Home Loan Mortgage Corporation (Freddie Mac).

Subtitle H - Reports and Data Collection

Section 9701

Directs the Comptroller General to study and report to Congress on certain interagency efforts to crackdown on mortgage foreclosure rescue scams and loan modification fraud in order to advise Congress on the risks and vulnerabilities of emerging schemes in the loan modification arena.

Section 9702

Amends the Helping Families Save Their Homes Act of 2009 to require certain mortgage data to be reported by state.

Subtitle I - Multifamily Mortgage Resolution

Section 9801

Directs the HUD Secretary to develop a program to ensure protection of current and future tenants and at-risk multifamily properties.

Subtitle J - Study of Effect of Drywall Presence on Foreclosures

(Sec. 9901) Directs the HUD Secretary to study and report to Congress regarding the effect upon residential mortgage loan foreclosures of: (1) the presence of drywall imported from China between 2004 and the end of 2007; and (2) the availability of property insurance for residential structures in which such drywall is present.

Subtitle K - Home Affordable Modification Program

Section 9911

Instructs the Secretary of the Treasury to revise the supplemental directives and other guidelines for the Home Affordable Modification Program of the Making Home Affordable initiative to require each mortgage servicer participating in such program to provide each borrower under a mortgage whose request for a mortgage modification under the Program is denied with all borrower-related and mortgage-related input data used in any net present value (NPV) analyses performed in connection with the subject mortgage. Requires such input data to be provided to the borrower at the time of such denial. Directs the Secretary to establish a public website that provides: (1) a calculator for NPV analyses of a mortgage, based on the Secretary's methodology for calculating such value, that mortgagors can use to enter information regarding their own mortgages; and (2) a determination after entering such information of whether such mortgage would be accepted or rejected for modification under the Program.

Subtitle L - Home Affordable Program

Section 9921

Instructs the Secretary of the Treasury to revise the guidelines for the Home Affordable Modification Program to make public the data being collected from each mortgage servicer and lender participating in the Program.

TITLE VIII - FORECLOSURE AVOIDANCE AND AFFORDABLE HOUSING

Section 10001

Directs the Secretary of the Treasury to transfer $3 billion in TARP funds to the HUD Secretary, which shall be credited to the Emergency Homeowners' Relief Fund for emergency mortgage assistance. Amends the Emergency Housing Act of 1975 to permit emergency mortgage assistance if the mortgagor has incurred a substantial reduction in income as a result of involuntary unemployment or underemployment due to medical conditions. Revises requirements for emergency mortgage assistance to replace the maximum amount of $250 per month with an amount determined reasonably necessary to supplement what the homeowner is capable of contributing toward the mortgage payment. Caps the aggregate amount of such assistance to any homeowner at $50,000. Makes the interest rate fixed for the life of an insured loan or credit advance. Limits the interest rate to that generally charged for HUD-insured mortgages on single-family housing. Prohibits the charging of any interest on deferred interest on such a loan or credit advance. Requires the Secretary, in establishing rates, terms, and conditions for loans or advances of credit, to take into account a homeowner's ability to repay such loan or credit advance. Authorizes any eligible homeowner who receives such a grant or credit advance to repay the loan in full, without penalty, by lump sum or by installment payments at any time before it becomes due and payable. Repeals the 40% cap on the total amount of loans and credit advances by a financial institution that may be insured, and the 90% cap on the payment of any single loss claim that may be paid out. Increases from $1.5 billion to $3 billion the cap on the aggregate amount of insured loans and advances, but includes emergency mortgage relief payments in such amount. Directs the Secretary to establish underwriting guidelines or procedures to allocate amounts made available for incurred loans and advances and for emergency relief payments, based on the likelihood that a mortgagor will be able to resume mortgage payments. Repeals the authorization of appropriations for the emergency mortgage relief program, but extends through FY2011 the authority to insure loans and credit advances under the program and to make emergency mortgage relief payments. Repeals the authority of each federal supervisory agency to waive or relax limitations pertaining to their operations with respect to mortgage delinquencies in order to cause or encourage forebearance in residential mortgage loan foreclosures. Repeals certain reporting requirements as well as the authority of the FDIC to make credit advances to insured banks to facilitate their participation in the emergency mortgage relief program.

Section 10002

Directs the Secretary of the Treasury to transfer to the HUD Secretary $1 billion to assist states and local government units for the redevelopment of abandoned and foreclosed homes.

Title IX - Nonadmitted and Reinsurance Reform Act

Nonadmitted and Reinsurance Reform Act of 2009 -

Subtitle A - Nonadmitted Insurance

Section 10101

Prohibits any state other than the home state of an insured from requiring a premium tax payment for nonadmitted insurance. Authorizes states to establish procedures to allocate among themselves the premium taxes paid to an insured's home state. Declares that Congress intends that each state adopt nationwide uniform requirements, forms, and procedures, such as an interstate compact, that provide for the reporting, payment, collection, and allocation of premium taxes for nonadmitted insurance consistent with this Act. Allows an insured's home state to require surplus lines brokers and certain insureds to file annual tax allocation reports detailing the portion of the nonadmitted insurance premiums attributable to properties, risks, or exposures located in each state.

Section 10102

Subjects nonadmitted insurance solely to the regulatory requirements of the insured's home state. Declares that only an insured's home state may require a surplus lines broker to be licensed to conduct nonadmitted insurance business with respect to such insured. Declares that state law, rule, or regulation that restricts the placement of workers' compensation insurance or excess insurance for self-funded workers' compensation plans with a nonadmitted insurer is not preempted.

Section 10103

Prohibits a state from collecting fees relating to licensure of a surplus lines broker in the state unless it has a regulatory mechanism in effect for participation in the national insurance producer database of the National Association of Insurance Commissioners (NAIC), or any other equivalent uniform national database.

Section 10104

Prohibits a state from establishing eligibility criteria for nonadmitted insurers domiciled in a U.S. jurisdiction except in conformance with the Non-Admitted Insurance Model Act, unless the state has adopted nationwide uniform requirements, forms, and procedures developed in accordance with this Act that include alternative nationwide uniform eligibility requirements. Prohibits a state from prohibiting a surplus lines broker from placing nonadmitted insurance with, or procuring nonadmitted insurance from, a nonadmitted insurer domiciled outside the United States and listed on the NAIC International Insurers Department Quarterly Listing of Alien Insurers.

Section 10105

Cites conditions with which a surplus lines broker seeking to procure or place nonadmitted insurance in a state for an exempt commercial purchaser must comply in order to win exemption from any state requirement to make a due diligence search to determine whether the full amount or type of insurance sought by such exempt commercial purchaser can be obtained from admitted insurers.

Section 10106

Requires the Comptroller General to study and report to Congress on the nonadmitted insurance market in order to determine the effect of this title upon the size and market share of the nonadmitted insurance market for providing coverage typically provided by the admitted insurance market.

Subtitle B - Reinsurance

Section 10201

Prohibits a state from denying credit for reinsurance for the insurer's ceded risk if the domiciliary state of an insurer purchasing reinsurance (the ceding insurer) recognizes such credit and: (1) is either an NAIC-accredited state, or (2) has financial solvency requirements substantially similar to NAIC accreditation requirements. Preempts the extraterritorial application of a non-domiciliary state's laws, regulations, or other actions (except those related to taxes and assessments on insurance companies or insurance income) to the extent that they: (1) restrict or eliminate the rights of the ceding insurer or the assuming insurer to resolve disputes pursuant to contractual arbitration that is not inconsistent with federal law; (2) require that a certain state's law shall govern the reinsurance contract, its requirements, or any disputes arising from it; or (3) attempt to enforce a reinsurance contract on terms different than those set forth in it, if those terms are not inconsistent with this subtitle.

Section 10202

Reserves to a reinsurer's domiciliary state sole responsibility for regulating the reinsurer's financial solvency if it is either NAIC-accredited, or has financial solvency requirements substantially similar to NAIC. Prohibits any other state from requiring a reinsurer to provide financial information in addition to that required by its NAIC-compliant domiciliary state.

Subtitle C - Rule of Construction

Section 10301

Prohibits any construction of this Act to modify, impair, or supersede the application of the antitrust laws. States that any implied or actual conflict between this Act and any amendments to this Act and the antitrust laws shall be resolved in favor of the operation of the antitrust laws.

TITLE X - INTEREST-BEARING TRANSACTION ACCOUNTS AUTHORIZED

Section 11001

Amends the Federal Reserve Act, the Home Owners' Loan Act, and the Federal Deposit Insurance Act to repeal the prohibition against the payment of interest on demand deposits.

In: Financial Crimes: Fraud, Theft... ISBN: 978-1-61122-479-5
Editors: Jonathan G. McDougal

Chapter 5

FINANCIAL CRIMES REPORT TO THE PUBLIC - FISCAL YEAR 2009

Federal Crimes Section, Federal Bureau of Investigation

FINANCIAL CRIMES

The Federal Bureau of Investigation (FBI) investigates matters relating to fraud, theft, or embezzlement occurring within or against the national and international financial community. These crimes are characterized by deceit, concealment, or violation of trust and are not dependent upon the application or threat of physical force or violence. Such acts are committed by individuals and organizations to obtain personal or business advantage. The FBI focuses its financial crimes investigations on such criminal activities as corporate fraud, securities and commodities fraud, health care fraud, financial institution fraud, mortgage fraud, insurance fraud, mass marketing fraud, and money laundering. These are the identified priority crime problem areas of the Financial Crimes Section (FCS) of the FBI.

The mission of the FCS is to oversee the investigation of financial fraud and to facilitate the forfeiture of assets from those engaging in federal crimes. In Fiscal Year (FY) 2009, the FCS was comprised of the Asset Forfeiture/Money Laundering Unit (AF/MLU), the Economic Crimes Unit (ECU), the Health Care Fraud Unit (HCFU), the Forensic Accountant Unit (FAU), and the National Mortgage Fraud Team (NMFT).

The ECU is responsible for significant frauds targeted against individuals, businesses, and industries to include: corporate fraud, insurance fraud (non-health care related), securities and commodities fraud, mass marketing fraud, telemarketing fraud, high yield investment schemes, Ponzi schemes, advance fees schemes, and pyramid schemes.

The HCFU oversees investigations targeting individuals and/or organizations who are defrauding public and private health care systems. Areas investigated under the HCFU include: billing for services not rendered, billing for a higher reimbursable service than performed (upcoding), performing unnecessary services, kickbacks, unbundling of tests and services to generate higher fees, durable medical equipment (DME) fraud, pharmaceutical drug diversion, outpatient surgery fraud, and Internet pharmacy sales.

The mission of the NMFT is to identify, target, disrupt, and dismantle criminal organizations and individuals who engage in fraud schemes which impact financial institutions particularly in the areas of mortgage fraud and bank failures.

The mission of the AF/MLU as it relates to financial institution fraud (FIF) is to identify, target, disrupt, and dismantle criminal organizations and individuals through the strategic use of asset forfeiture; and to ensure that field offices employ the money laundering violation in all investigations, where appropriate, to assist in the disruption and/or dismantlement of criminal enterprises.

The AF/MLU also has responsibilities for the management of the Forfeiture Support Project (FSP) in Calverton, Maryland. Although the FSP's mission is closely tied to that of the AF/MLU, it does have a separate mission statement which is documented as follows: The mission of the FSP is to support the forfeiture component of all major FBI investigations through data entry and analysis of financial documents, forensic accounting, and tracing assets subject to forfeiture.

The FAU was established in March 2009 to support all FBI investigative matters requiring a forensic financial investigation. The FAU provides oversight of the Forensic Accountant (FoA) and Financial Analyst (FA) Programs, ensuring that the FBI's financial investigative needs and priorities are continuously addressed. Key to the FAU's mission is developing, managing, and enhancing the FoA and FA Programs, to ensure that FBI financial investigative matters are expedited with the high level of expertise required in an increasingly complex global financial system.

Based upon field office crime surveys, current trends in the White Collar Crime (WCC) arena, and directives established by the President, the Attorney General, the Director, and the Criminal Investigative Division (CID), the following national priorities for the WCC Program (WCCP) have been established: public corruption, corporate fraud/securities fraud, health care fraud, FIF (to include bank failures and mortgage fraud), money laundering, insurance fraud, and mass marketing fraud.

Although public corruption is a national priority within the WCCP, it will not be addressed in this chapter. Each section of this chapter provides an overview, statistical accomplishments, and case examples of the identified priority crime problems specifically addressed by the FCS. Where appropriate, suggestions are made in order to protect the public from being victimized by fraudulent activity.

CORPORATE FRAUD

I. General Overview

As the lead agency investigating corporate fraud, the FBI has focused its efforts on cases which involve accounting schemes, self-dealing by corporate executives, and obstruction of justice. The majority of corporate fraud cases pursued by the FBI involve accounting schemes designed to deceive investors, auditors, and analysts about the true financial condition of a corporation. Through the manipulation of financial data, the share price of a corporation remains artificially inflated based on fictitious performance indicators provided to the investing public. In addition to significant financial losses to investors, corporate fraud has the potential to cause immeasurable damage to the U.S. economy and investor confidence.

While the number of cases involving the falsification of financial information remains relatively stable, the FBI has observed a spike in the number of corporate fraud cases involving subprime lending institutions, brokerage houses, home-building firms, hedge funds and financial institutions, as a result of the financial crisis partly caused by the collapse of the subprime mortgage market in the fall of 2007. As a result of the current financial crisis, trillions of dollars in shareholder value have been lost, several prominent companies, i.e., Lehman Brothers, have gone out of business, several prominent banks, i.e., IndyMac Bank and Washington Mutual, have failed, and the Federal Government has provided over a trillion dollars in relief to keep other companies from failing, i.e., American Insurance Group, General Motors, and CitiGroup.

A subprime mortgage lender is a business that lends to borrowers who do not qualify for loans from mainstream lenders. Once the subprime loans have been issued, they are bundled and sold as securities -- a process known as securitization. Fraud has been identified throughout the loan process, which commences with the borrower providing false information to the mortgage broker and/or lender. The next layer of potential fraud, the corporate fraud, occurs with the banks, brokerage houses, and other financial institutions that package loans through the securitization process. As the housing market declined, subprime lenders have been forced to buy back a number of nonperforming loans. Many of these subprime lenders have relied on a continuous increase in real estate values to allow the borrowers to refinance or sell their properties before going into default. However, based on the sales slowdown in the housing market, loan defaults increased, the secondary market for subprime securities dwindled, and the securities lost value. As a result, publicly traded stocks dramatically decreased in value as financial institutions realized large losses due to the sub prime securities they held or insured, resulting in financial difficulties and bankruptcies.

As publicly traded companies suffered financial difficulties due to subprime market, analyses of company financials have identified instances of false accounting entries and fraudulently inflated assets and revenues. Investigations have determined that several of these companies manipulated their reported loan portfolio risks and used various accounting schemes to inflate their financial reports. In addition, before these companies' stocks rapidly declined in value, executives with insider information sold their equity positions and profited illegally. The FBI is working with the U.S. Department of Justice (DOJ), the U.S. Securities and Exchange Commission (SEC), and other U.S. regulatory agencies to identify possible corporate fraud centered on violations of insider trading, securities fraud, and accounting fraud.

In addition to the subprime market issue, corporate fraud matters involving seal-dealing by corporate executives, particularly utilizing companies to perpetrate large-scale Ponzi fraud schemes, continue to be an issue of concern. Traditionally, Ponzi schemes were perpetrated by individuals, or small groups, within a community environment. However, the current financial crisis resulted in the exposure of several large Ponzi schemes perpetrated not on an individual community level, but on a corporate national level by executives of what were once considered legitimate companies, i.e., Petters Company, Inc. (see page 8).

Corporate fraud remains one of the highest priorities for the FBI. At the end of 2009, 592 corporate fraud cases were being pursued by FBI field offices throughout the United States, several of which involved losses to public investors that individually exceed $1 billion.

Corporate fraud investigations involve the following activities:

(1) Falsification of financial information, including:
  (a) False accounting entries;
  (b) Bogus trades designed to inflate profit or hide losses; and,
  (c) False transactions designed to evade regulatory oversight.
(2) Self-dealing by corporate insiders, including:
  (a) Insider trading;
  (b) Kickbacks;
  (c) Backdating of executive stock options;
  (d) Misuse of corporate property for personal gain; and,
  (e) Individual tax violations related to self-dealing.
(3) Obstruction of justice designed to conceal any of the above-noted types of criminal conduct, particularly when the obstruction impedes the inquiries of the SEC, other regulatory agencies, and/or law enforcement agencies.

The FBI has formed partnerships with numerous agencies to capitalize on their expertise in specific areas such as securities, tax, pensions, energy, and commodities. The FBI has placed greater emphasis on investigating allegations of these frauds by working closely with the SEC, Financial Industry Regulation Authority (FINRA), Internal Revenue Service (IRS), Department of Labor, Federal Energy Regulatory Commission, Commodity Futures Trading Commission (CFTC), U.S. Postal Inspection Service (USPIS), and Special Inspector General for the Troubled Asset Relief Program (SIGTARP). In addition, the FBI is an active member of the Financial Fraud Enforcement Task Force (FFETF) created by Presidential Executive Order in November 2009. As reflected in the statistical accomplishments of the FBI, the cooperative and multiagency investigative approach has resulted in highly successful prosecutions.

The FBI has also worked with numerous organizations in the private industry to increase public awareness about combating corporate fraud, to include: Public Company Accounting Oversight Board, American Institute of

Certified Public Accountants, Association of Certified Fraud Examiners, and the North American Securities Administrator's Association, Inc. These organizations have been able to provide referrals for expert witnesses and other technical assistance regarding accounting and securities issues. In addition, the Financial Crimes Enforcement Network (FinCEN) and Dun & Bradstreet have been able to provide significant background information on subject individuals and/or subject companies to further investigative efforts.

II. Overall Accomplishments

Through FY 2009, cases pursued by the FBI resulted in 153 indictments/informations and 156 convictions of corporate criminals. Numerous cases are pending plea agreements and trials. During FY 2009, the FBI secured $6.1 billion in restitution orders and $5.4 million in fines from corporate criminals. The chart below reflects corporate fraud pending cases from FY 2005 through FY 2009 as follows: FY 2005— 423 cases; FY 2006—486 cases; FY 2007—529 cases; FY 2008—545 cases; and FY 2009—592 cases.

III. Significant Cases

Petters Company, Inc. (Minneapolis): Thomas J. Petters, through his company, Petters Group Worldwide LLC (PGW), obtained loans from hedge funds and investment groups for the stated purpose of financing sales to well-known big box retailers, such as Costco and Sam's Club. The investigation revealed that the purchase and subsequent sale of merchandise to the retailers were actually fabricated transactions supported by fictional documentation. Thomas J. Petters was indicted for mail and wire fraud, conspiracy, and money laundering in December 2008 for his role in a $3.4 billion corporate fraud scheme. Six individuals have been indicted during the course of the investigation for various roles in the scheme, including the production of false banking transaction documentation. Petters' trial began on October 28, 2009, and Petters was convicted on December 2, 2009, following an 18-day trial, on all counts of the indictment. It is anticipated that Petters will be sentenced sometime in 2010.

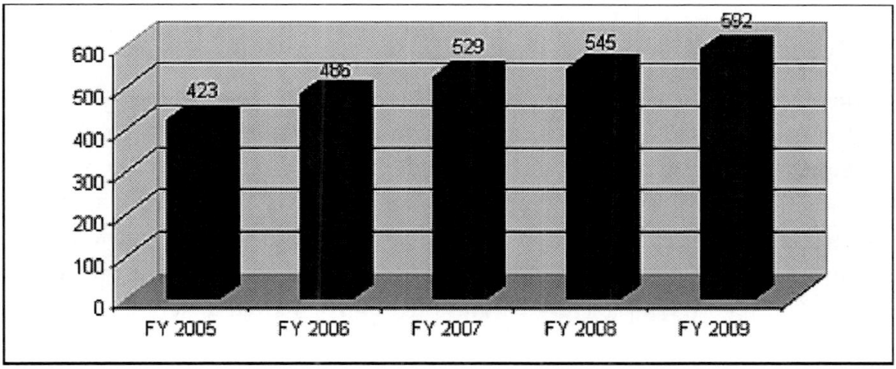

Corporate Fraud Pending Cases

Credit Suisse (New York): Credit Suisse is a global financial services company, advising clients across the globe in all aspects of finance. ST Microelectronics (STM) is a Switzerland-based semiconductor company with annual net revenue of US $9.85 billion in 2006. In 2006, STM invested $400 million with Credit Suisse in what were purportedly securities backed by student loans (to include investment statements); however, the funds were backed with subprime loans. Credit Suisse tried unsuccessfully to settle the matter for $280 million. The two managers, Eric Butler and Julian Tzolov, were indicted on securities fraud charges and arrested in June 2008. Tzolov pled guilty and testified as a key witness for the government in the trial against Butler. After several weeks of trial, Butler was convicted in August 2009 by the jury and later sentenced to five years in prison. It is anticipated that Tzolov will be sentenced in 2010.

1031 Tax Group (Richmond): From August 2005 through April 2007, Edward Okun, former owner of 1031 Tax Group LLP (1031 Tax Group) and Investment Properties of America (IPofA), and Lara Coleman, former Chief Financial Officer (CFO) of IPofA, and two other conspirators used 1031 Tax Group and its subsidiaries in a scheme to defraud clients through false pretenses. Section 1031 of the Internal Revenue Code allows investment property owners to defer the capital gains tax that would otherwise be due on properties sold, dependant on the use of the proceeds to purchase new property in a specified time frame. Okun and Coleman obtained funds by promising clients their money would be used solely to effect 1031 exchanges as outlined in the exchange agreements. After making such promises, Okun and Coleman misappropriated approximately $132 million in client funds to support Okun's lavish lifestyle, pay operating expenses for his various companies, invest in commercial real estate, and purchase additional qualified intermediary companies to obtain access to additional client funds. Okun and Coleman also instructed employees to withdraw cash from a company bank account and smuggle the cash to Okun's personal yacht on Paradise Island in the Bahamas to avoid federal currency reporting requirements. The two additional conspirators, Robert D. Field II and Richard E. Simring, were the CFO and Chief Legal Officer, respectively, of a holding company set up to oversee both IPofA and the 1031 Tax Group. Both pled guilty and were sentenced to five years and three years, respectively. After pleading guilty, Coleman was sentenced to 10 years in prison. Okun received a prison sentence of 100 years after he was found guilty at trial.

Securities and Commodities Fraud

I. General Overview

The recent financial crisis saw the Dow Jones Industrial Average fall from its high of 14,164 in October 2007 to 6,547 in March 2009. As a result, the FBI witnessed a prolific rise in Ponzi and other High Yield Investment Fraud (HYIF) schemes as the frauds were exposed as investors sought redemptions. With the development of new schemes, such as securities market manipulation via cyber intrusion, and the trend in exposure of Ponzi schemes due to market deterioration, securities and commodities fraud is on the rise. Over the last five years, open securities and commodities fraud investigations have increased by 33 percent. During this time period, the losses associated with these types of schemes have increased to billions of dollars.

The continuing integration of global capital markets has created unprecedented opportunities for U.S. businesses to access capital and investors to diversify their portfolios. Whether through college savings plans or retirement accounts (e.g. 401k plans), more and more Americans are choosing to invest in the U.S. securities and commodities markets. A 2008 joint study by the Securities Industry and Financial Markets Association and Investment Company Institute suggests that approximately 47 percent of U.S. households participate in the market through equity or bond ownership, up from 39 percent in 1989. This large-scale investment growth, however, has also led to significant growth in the amount of fraud and misconduct seen in these markets. The creation of diversified investment vehicles and the tremendous increase in theamount of money being invested have created greater opportunities for individuals and businesses to perpetrate fraudulent investment schemes.

New opportunities for fraud have also developed in response to government programs that were established to support the financial markets. The FBI anticipates new iterations of traditional fraud schemes to develop as a result of the government-spending programs such as the Troubled Asset Relief Program and the Termed Asset-Backed Securities Loan Facility. As such, combating securities and commodities frauds remains a top priority for the FBI.

The losses are associated with depreciative market value of businesses, reduced or nonexistent return on investments, and legal and investigative costs. The victims of securities and commodities frauds include individual investors, financial institutions, public and private companies, government entities, and retirement funds.

Now more than ever, the well-being of the global economy rests on the diligent enforcement of laws and regulations designed to ensure the fair and orderly operation of the capital markets. The FBI is not only cognizant of this critical requirement, but is uniquely positioned to help meet the U.S. Government's criminal investigative responsibilities in this area.

The FBI works closely with various governmental and private entities to investigate and prevent fraudulent activity in the securities markets. In an effort to help bolster these relationships and optimize workforce needs, many FBI field offices operate task forces and working groups with other law enforcement and regulatory agencies. These agencies include the SEC, U. S. Attorney's Office (USAO), CFTC, FINRA, USPIS, and the IRS. Cooperation among agencies helps the FBI address the problem of securities and commodities fraud more effectively and allows the FBI to more efficiently allocate its resources.

At the end of FY 2009, the FBI was investigating 1,510 cases of securities and commodities fraud and had 177 Special Agents assigned to address this crime problem. Following are brief descriptions of some of the most prevalent types of fraud being encountered today:

Market Manipulation: These schemes, commonly referred to as "Pump and Dumps," are effected by creating artificial buying pressure for a targeted security, generally a low-trading volume issuer in the over-the-counter securities market that is largely controlled by the fraud perpetrators. This artificially increased trading volume has the effect of artificially increasing the price of the targeted security (i.e., the Pump), which is rapidly sold off into the inflated market for the security by the fraud perpetrators (i.e., the Dump); resulting in illicit gains to the perpetrators and losses to innocent third party investors. Typically, the increased trading volume is generated by inducing unwitting investors to purchase shares of the targeted security through false or deceptive sales practices and/or public information releases.

A modern variation on these schemes involves largely foreign-based computer criminals gaining unauthorized access and intruding into the online brokerage accounts of unsuspecting victims in the United States. These intruded victim accounts are then utilized to engage in coordinated online purchases of the targeted security to affect manipulation, while the fraud perpetrators sell their preexisting holdings in the targeted security into the inflated market.

High Yield Investment Fraud: HYIF schemes may take many forms but are all characterized by offers of low or no risk investments that guarantee unusually high rates of return. Most common among this type of fraud are the following schemes:

The Ponzi Scheme—Named after its early 20th century creator, Charles Ponzi, these schemes use money collected from new 'investors' (i.e., victims), rather than profits from the purported underlying business venture, to pay the high rates of return promised to earlier victims. This arrangement gives victims the impression that there is a legitimate, money-making enterprise behind the perpetrator's story when, in reality, victim monies are the only source of funding.

The Pyramid Scheme—As in Ponzi Schemes, the money collected from newer victims of the fraud is paid to earlier victims to provide a veneer of legitimacy. In Pyramid Schemes, however, the victims themselves are induced to recruit further victims through the payment of recruitment commissions.

Prime Bank Scheme—Victims are induced to invest in financial instruments, allegedly issued by well-known institutions, which offer risk-free opportunities for high rates of return; benefits which are allegedly the result of the perpetrator's access to a secret worldwide exchange ordinarily open only to the world's largest financial institutions.

Advance Fee Fraud: This category of fraud encompasses a broad variety of schemes which are designed to induce their victims into remitting up-front payments in exchange for the promise of goods, services, and/or prizes. In the securities and commodities fraud context, victims are informed that in order to participate in a promising investment opportunity, they must first pay various taxes and/or fees. Advance fee fraud schemes are further discussed in the mass marketing fraud section of this chapter.

Hedge Fund Fraud: Hedge funds are private investment partnerships which have historically accepted only high-net worth clients willing to meet significant minimum investment thresholds. The industry as a whole has been largely unregulated but has become increasingly relevant to middle class investors through their exposure to hedge fund activities via ancillary investments (e.g., pension funds). The relative lack of regulatory scrutiny has made the industry vulnerable to fraud by fund managers, to include overstatement/misappropriation of fund assets; overcharging for fund management fees; insider trading; market timing; and late trading.

Commodities Fraud: These schemes typically involve the deceptive or fraudulent sale of commodities investments. In such instances, false or deceptive sales practices are used to solicit victim funds for commodities transactions that either never occur or are inconsistent with the original sales pitches. Alternatively, commodities market participants may attempt to illegally manipulate the market for a commodity by such actions as fraudulently reporting price information or cornering the market to artificially increase the price of the targeted commodity.

Foreign Exchange Fraud: These schemes are characterized by the use of false or deceptive sales practices, alleging high rates of return for minimal risk, to induce victims to invest in the foreign currency exchange market. In such instances, the touted transactions never occur, are inconsistent with the original sales pitches, or are executed for the sole purpose of generating excessive trading commissions in breach of fiduciary responsibilities to the victim client. Alternatively, individual corrupt currency traders employed by large financial institutions may attempt to manipulate foreign currency exchange prices in an effort to generate illicit trading profits for their own enrichment.

Broker Embezzlement: These schemes involve illicit and unauthorized actions by brokers to steal directly from their clients. Such schemes may be facilitated by the forging of client documents, doctoring of account statements, unauthorized trading/funds transfer activities, or other conduct in breach of the broker's fiduciary responsibilities to the victim client.

Late-Day Trading: These schemes involve the illicit purchase and sale of securities after regular market hours. Such trading is restricted in order to prevent individuals from profiting on market-moving information which is released after the close of regular trading. Unscrupulous traders attempt to illegally exploit such opportunities by buying or selling securities at the market close price, secure in the knowledge that the market-moving information will generate illicit profits at the opening of trading on the following day.

II. Overall Accomplishments

As of the end of FY 2009, the FBI was investigating 1,510 cases of securities and commodities fraud and had already recorded 412 indictments/informations and 306 convictions. Additional notable accomplishments in FY 2009 include: $8.1 billion in restitution orders; $63.4 million in recoveries; $12.8 million in fines; and $126 million in seizures. The chart below reflects securities and commodities fraud pending cases from FY 2005 through FY 2009 as follows: FY 2005—1,139 cases; FY 2006—1,165 cases; FY 2007—1,217 cases; FY 2008—1,210 cases; and FY 2009— 1,510 cases.

III. Significant Cases

Bernard L. Madoff Investment Securities (New York): This investigation centered on Bernard L. Madoff, founder of BLM Investment Services LLC (BLMIS), who was arrested in December 2008 on charges of securities fraud. The complaint charged Madoff with running a $64 billion Ponzi scheme. Madoff is the founder of BLMIS, a securities broker dealer, and former Chairman of the NASDAQ Stock Market. Madoff made statements to his employees that his business was a giant Ponzi scheme and that the business had been insolvent for years. Madoff provided clients with monthly investment statements and trade confirmation for transactions that never actually occurred. For decades, Madoff has utilized new client funds to pay profits and redemptions to existing clients. Madoff pled guilty to the indictment and was sentenced to 150 years in prison in June 2009. Thus far, nearly $1 billion in property and assets have been seized, of which approximately $750 million have been forfeited.

Richard Monroe Harkless, dba MX Factors LLC (Los Angeles): This investigation centered on Richard Monroe Harkless who operated a Ponzi scheme from 2000 through 2003 via his company MX Factors. Harkless informed clients that he was investing their money in government-guaranteed construction loans, which provided returns as high as 14 percent every three months. In reality, Harkless diverted the investor funds to Belize and Mexico to pay for personal expenses. Hundreds of individuals invested more than $60 million, with losses in excess of $39 million. The losses by individual investors ranged from $10,000 to more than $500,000. In September 2009, Harkless was sentenced to more than 100 years in prison. This investigation was worked jointly with the IRS and USPIS.

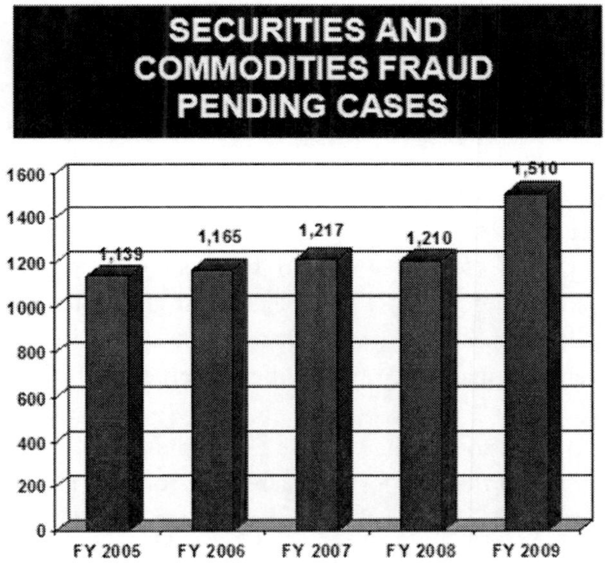

Curtis Somoza (Los Angeles): This investigation centered on Curtis Somoza who ran an investment scheme whereby 63 California and Texas investors were defrauded out of $64 million. Somoza guaranteed large returns for investments in a bond-trading program and life insurance pool that would benefit churches in South Los Angeles. Somoza was convicted in 2008 and was sentenced in November 2009 to 25 years in prison for his involvement in this large investment scheme.

HEALTH CARE FRAUD

I. General Overview

The FBI's mission in the area of health care fraud (HCF) is to oversee the FBI's HCF initiatives by providing national guidance and assistance to support HCF investigations targeting individuals and organizations who are defrauding the public and private health care systems. The FBI, along with its federal, state, and local law enforcement partners, the Centers for Medicare and Medicaid Services (CMS), and other government and privately sponsored program participants, work closely together to address vulnerabilities, fraud, and abuse.

All health care programs are subject to fraud; however, Medicare and Medicaid programs are the most visible. Estimates of fraudulent billings to health care programs, both public and private, are estimated between three and ten percent of total health care expenditures. The fraud schemes are not specific to any area, but they are found throughout the entire country. The schemes target large health care programs, public and private, as well as beneficiaries. Certain schemes tend to be worked more often in certain geographical areas, and certain ethnic or national groups tend to also employ the same fraud schemes. The fraud schemes have, over time, become more sophisticated and complex and are now being perpetrated by more organized crime groups.

HCF is expected to continue to rise as people live longer. This increase will produce a greater demand for Medicare benefits. As a result, it is expected that the utilization of long and short-term care facilities such as skilled nursing, assisted living, and hospice services will expand substantially in the future. Additionally, fraudulent billings and medically unnecessary services billed to health care insurers are prevalent throughout the country. These activities are becoming increasingly complex and can be perpetrated by corporate-driven schemes and systematic abuse by providers.

The most recent CMS statistical estimates project the total health care expenditures will total $2.26 trillion, representing 16.2 percent of the Gross Domestic Product (GDP). By the year 2016, CMS estimates total health care spending to exceed $4.14 trillion, representing 19.6 percent of the GDP.

With health care expenditures rising at over twice the rate of inflation, it is especially important to coordinate all investigative efforts to combat fraud within the health care system. The FBI is the primary investigative agency in the fight against HCF, and has jurisdiction over both the federal and private insurance programs. With more than $1 trillion being spent in the private sector on health care and its related services, the FBI's efforts are crucial to the success of the overall program. The FBI leverages its resources in both the private and public arenas through investigative partnerships with agencies such as the U.S. Department of Health and Human Services-Office of Inspector General (HHS-OIG), the Food and Drug Administration (FDA), Drug Enforcement Agency (DEA), Defense Criminal Investigative Service, Office of Personnel Management, IRS-CID, and various state and local agencies. On the private side, the FBI is actively involved with national groups, such as the National Health Care Anti-Fraud Association (NHCAA), the National Insurance Crime Bureau (NICB), the Blue Cross and Blue Shield Association (BCBSA), the American Association of Retired Persons, and the Coalition Against Insurance Fraud, as well as many other professional and grass-roots efforts to expose and investigate fraud within the system.

In furtherance of the FBI's efforts to combat HCF in the United States, the FBI participates in various initiatives with federal, state, and local agencies. At the Headquarters level, the FBI participates in a Senior Level Working Group which includes the CMS, DOJ, HHS-OIG, and other agencies to identify and assess health care industry vulnerabilities and make recommendations to protect the industry and the public through a coordinated effort. At the Headquarters level, the FBI is also involved in biweekly coordination meetings at the DOJ which includes various DOJ components involved in the fight against HCF. National-level liaison is also maintained with the DEA, FDA, Bureau of Immigration and Customs Enforcement (ICE), BCBSA, and other partners.

Throughout the country, FBI field offices participate in HCF Working Groups which involve law enforcement agencies, prosecutors, regulatory agencies, and health insurance industry professionals to identify the various crime problems involving HCF. The FBI develops national and local initiatives when large-scale fraud is detected, which may involve participation by several FBI field offices and other law enforcement agencies.

Over the years, FBI national initiatives have addressed frauds involving medical transportation, DME, hospital cost reporting, outpatient surgery centers, pharmaceutical fraud, and a variety of other specialized investigations. FBI offices also establish state and local initiatives to meet the needs of the community. Throughout the country, various field offices have conducted their own initiatives targeting clinic, pharmacy, medical equipment, home health agency, cosmetic surgery center, and other frauds which are of great concern within a community. The FBI participates in task forces whenever possible to address specific crime problems or groups of individuals. In order to meet the needs of the private insurance industry, the FBI works very closely with the NHCAA to identify crime trends and provide training to industry and law enforcement agency personnel. Most of the insurance companies utilize an internal Special Investigations Unit, which works closely with the FBI and our law enforcement partners.

HCF investigations are among the highest priority investigations within the FBI's WCCP, ranking behind only public corruption and corporate fraud. National initiatives include the DME Fraud Initiative, the Infusion Therapy Fraud Initiative, and the Home Health Care Fraud Initiative (HHCFI). Furthermore, numerous FBI field offices throughout the United States have proactively addressed significant crime problems through coordinated initiatives, task forces, and undercover operations to identify and pursue investigations against the most egregious offenders, which may include organized criminal activity and criminal enterprises. Organized criminal activity has been identified in the operation of medical clinics, independent diagnostic testing facilities, DME, and other health care facilities. The FBI is committed to addressing this criminal activity through disruption, dismantlement, and prosecution of criminal organizations. One of the most significant trends observed in recent HCF cases includes the willingness of medical professionals to risk patient harm in their schemes. FBI investigations in several offices are focusing on subjects who conduct unnecessary surgeries, prescribe dangerous drugs without medical necessity, and engage in abusive or sub-standard care practices. Recent trends also suggest that advances in technology and electronic medical data have caused HCF schemes to evolve. The FBI has developed a significant amount of expertise in investigating technical schemes involving medical data theft and other fraud schemes facilitated through the use of computers. Of course, fraud schemes continue to consist of traditional schemes that involve fraudulent billing, such as billing for services not rendered and upcoding of charges for services provided.

In December 2006, the DME Initiative was developed to address the significant crime problem associated with DME providers. Information developed with assistance from the CMS, the NHCAA, and the FBI's Financial Crimes Intelligence Unit (FCIU) identified DME providers as one of the top two provider types identified within all case referrals, preliminary investigations, and suspensions. The initiative was established to bring additional attention to DME fraud and the FBI's commitment to addressing the crime problem. The primary goal of the initiative is to provide intelligence to field offices concerning suspect DME providers, focusing on cases involving multiple districts or divisions, unique schemes, advanced techniques, and/or substantial loss amounts.

Infusion therapy fraud was established in April 2008. Its focus is on the billing of infusion-related services and medications that were not provided or were not medically necessary. An infusion is a method of intravenously introducing some substance into the human body. Receiving an infusion is more commonly referred to as "receiving an IV." In infusion therapy fraud, most often the perpetrator bills insurance providers for expensive medications that are rarely, if ever, administered to patients. In many cases, the medications are extremely powerful drugs used in only a small number of patients and require extensive management by a physician.

The HHCFI, established in January 2010, is the newest of the initiatives. Home health care makes up approximately $15.1 billion of the health care market and continues to grow. The expanding market is a target for perpetrators who are seeking to acquire a more significant share of illicit proceeds by exploiting expensive Home Health Agency (HHA) services. One of the more common HHA schemes, representing $4.5 billion and 30 percent of the overall industry, involves HHA providers who are inflating HHA diabetic episodes to create outlier payments which are in excess of the national 60-day episode payments. This scheme is projected to cost Medicare $1 billion in 2009, according to the CMS.

The Medicare Prescription Drug Program (Part D), implemented on January 1, 2006, has become an increasing focus and concern for the FBI. Prior to the implementation date, FBI Headquarters personnel regularly met with representatives from CMS and DOJ to share information, as well as review fraud and abuse occurring during the enrollment period. After the implementation date, the FBI established a working group for Part D which includes representatives from CMS, DOJ, HHS-OIG, FDA, DEA, USPIS, and the FTC. This working group shares and discusses information which can be used by each agency in future investigations of fraud related to this program. The FBI has worked with CMS to obtain regional training for field office personnel of the various agencies represented in this working group. The FBI is also working through CMS to maintain dialogue with the Medicare Drug Integrity Contractors (MEDICs) who have been tasked by CMS to identify, review, and analyze cases of suspected fraud and abuse in the Part D Program.

During the past year, the FBI continued to identify and analyze industry fraud trends through input from private and public health care program experts. Present areas of concern include DME, hospital fraud, physician fraud, home health agencies, beneficiary-sharing, chiropractic, pain management, and associated drug diversion, physical therapists, prescription drugs, multidisciplinary fraud, and identity theft which involve physician identifiers used to fraudulently bill government and private insurance programs.

As part of our national strategy to address HCF, the FBI cooperates with the DOJ and the various USAOs throughout the country to pursue offenders through parallel criminal and civil remedies. These cases typically target large-scale medical providers, such as hospitals and corporations, who engage in criminal activity and commit fraud against the Government which undermines the credibility of the health care system. As a result, a great deal of emphasis is placed on recovering the illegal proceeds through seizure and forfeiture proceedings, as well as substantial civil settlements. Upon the successful conviction of HCF offenders, the FBI provides assistance to various regulatory and state agencies, which may seek exclusion of convicted medical providers from further participation in the Medicare and Medicaid health care systems.

The FBI and the health care industry continue to expand their technology and intelligence assessments through the use of sophisticated data-mining techniques to identify patterns of fraud, systemic weaknesses, and aberrant billing activity.

In 2005, the FCS developed the Electronic Bank Records Initiative (EBRI). The EBRI was implemented to identify and develop a process for obtaining electronic (digital format) records from financial institutions. Historically, financial institutions have provided paper copies of records to law enforcement when they receive a subpoena from the government. These records are generally maintained by the banks in an electronic format. The time it takes the financial institution to make the copies of the records and for the investigative agencies to return the paper copies back to an electronic format for financial analysis creates a severe negative effect on the timeliness, effectiveness, and efficiency of investigations. In an effort to increase the efficiency of the process, a subpoena attachment was developed by the DOJ, FBI, and the IRS-CID for the production of electronic records instead of paper copies. The development included significant coordination with the financial institutions and their associations. The subpoena attachment was not based upon new or expanded laws, regulations, or rules. The attachment is merely meant to standardize and clarify the requests for electronic records according to the current Federal Rules of Criminal and Civil Procedure. In general terms, if a financial institution maintains records electronically, the requesting agency would be seeking to obtain the records electronically. In addition, the scope of the records requested has not changed due to the subpoena attachment, with the exception of seeking the records electronically.

The subpoena attachment was disseminated to FBI offices, IRS offices, and throughout the DOJ in November 2007. The goal of the DOJ, FBI, and IRS-CID is to inform and prepare financial institutions and their respective agencies for the use and response to the subpoena attachment. This includes working with financial institutions during the transition period in coordinating the requests and associated responses to subpoenas. In addition, it is anticipated the EBRI will greatly increase the efficiency of the financial records production process and provide significant costs savings to both the government and private industry.

II. Overall Accomplishments

Through FY 2009, 2,494 cases investigated by the FBI resulted in 945 indictments and 640 convictions of HCF criminals. It should be noted that numerous cases are pending plea agreements and trials. The following notable statistical accomplishments are reflective in FY 2009 for HCF: $1.6 billion in restitutions, $853 million in recoveries, $68 million in fines, and $54 million in seizures. The chart below reflects HCF pending cases from FY 2005 through FY 2009 as follows: FY 2005—2,547 cases; FY 2006—2,423 cases; FY 2007—2,493 cases; FY 2008—2,434 cases; and FY 2009—2,494 cases.

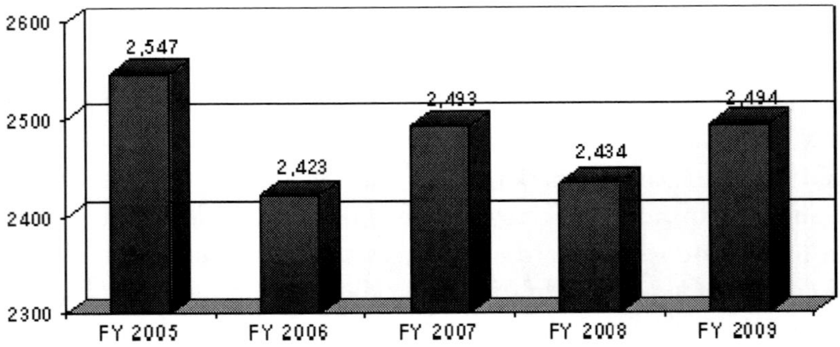

III. Significant Cases

Dr. Hany M. Iskander (Cleveland): Dr. Hany M. Iskander, an Egyptian national here on work visa, executed a scheme to defraud Medicare, Medicaid, and other health care benefit programs through his pain management business located in Bucyrus, Ohio, and Lewis Center, Ohio. The scheme involved millions of dollars of fraudulent claims for payment for medical services which were either not performed or which had no medical necessity to be performed. On October 2, 2009, Dr. Iskander and his wife, Evat Hanna, were found guilty of obstruction of justice by shredding and concealing medical records to impede a federal investigation. Pursuant to a plea agreement, Dr. Iskander agreed to serve at least 51 months' imprisonment to be determined by the sentencing judge, at a hearing set for February 2, 2010. Iskander also agreed to forfeit his medical license and to be deported to Egypt following his release from prison. The government has entered into a plea agreement with Iskander's wife recommending a sentence of home detention for one year, following which she will also be deported.

Pfizer Inc. (Boston): Investigation was predicated in August 2004 upon the receipt of qui tam information from the FDA that Pfizer employees may have destroyed records sought in a federal civil investigation and that company employees had been engaged in a series of transactions involving off-label promotions and kickbacks. Between 2001 and 2005, Pfizer northeast regional manager Mary Holloway directed approximately 100 sales employees to market the painkiller Valdecoxib (Bextra) for uses specifically prohibited by the FDA. On March 30, 2009, Holloway pled by criminal information to one count of distribution of a misbranded drug. Holloway was sentenced to 24 months' probation and a $75,000 fine on June 18, 2009. Holloway is the second subject convicted in this case. Thomas Farina, a New York-area sales manager for Pfizer was indicted in March 2008, and pled guilty to obstruction later that month. In January 2009, Pfizer agreed to pay the U.S. Government $2.3 billion to settle claims involving the drugs Bextra, Zyvox, Goedon, and Lyrica. Valdecoxib (Bextra) was a nonsteroidal anti-inflammatory prescription drug, administered in tablet form, which was used in the treatment of arthritis, inflammation, pain, and menstrual symptoms. Bextra was approved by the FDA for distribution in the United States in 2001. Pfizer withdrew Bextra from the U.S. market in 2005, after the FDA cited increased incidence of heart attacks, strokes, and serious skin reactions to the drug.

Operation Therascam (Miami): This HCF investigation was a large-scale joint investigation between the FBI, the HHS-OIG, USAO, Southern District of Florida, and DOJ trial attorneys from D.C. It was predicated on companies offering kickbacks to individuals who had access to patients residing in assisted living facilities for the purpose of billing for fraudulent claims to the Medicare program. During the initial stage of the investigation, a massive kickback network was uncovered involving a multitude of patients, physicians, DME companies, and pharmacies. The case led to more than 20 search warrants over the last several years, and the investigation resulted in more than 200 consensual recordings which resulted in the recovery of over $100,000 in kickback payments.

IV. Health Care Fraud Schemes

HCF is carried out by many segments of the health care system using various methods. Some of the most prevalent schemes include:

Billing for Services not Rendered—These schemes can have several meanings and could include any of the following:

- No medical service of any kind was rendered.
- The service was not rendered as described in the claim for payment.
- The service was previously billed and the claim had been paid.

Upcoding of Services—This type of scheme involves a billing practice where the health care provider submits a bill using a procedure code that yields a higher payment than the code for the service that was truly rendered. The upcoding of services varies according to the provider type. Examples of service upcoding include:

- A routine, follow-up doctor's office visit being billed as an initial or comprehensive office visit.
- Group therapy being billed as individual therapy.
- Unilateral procedures being billed as bilateral procedures.
- 30-minute sessions being billed as 50+ minute sessions.

Upcoding of Items—A medical supplier is upcoding when, for example, the supplier delivers to the patient a basic, manually propelled wheelchair, but bills the patient's health insurance plan for a more expensive motorized version of the wheelchair.

Duplicate Claims—A duplicate claim usually involves a certain item or service for which two claims are filed. In this scheme, an exact copy of the claim is not filed a second time; rather, the provider usually changes a portion, most often the date of service on the claim so that the health insurer will not realize the claim is a duplicate. In other words, the exact claim is not filed twice, but one service is billed two times, in an attempt to be paid twice for one service.

Unbundling—This is the practice of submitting bills in a fragmented fashion in order to maximize the reimbursement for various tests or procedures that are required to be billed together at a reduced cost. For example, clinical laboratory tests may be ordered individually, or in a "panel" (i.e., a lipid panel, an arthritis panel, a hepatitis panel). Billing tests within each panel as though they were done individually on subsequent days is an example of unbundling.

Excessive Services—These schemes typically involve the provision of medical services or items which are in excess of the patient's actual needs. Examples of excessive services include:

- A medical supply company delivering and billing for 30 wound care kits per week for a nursing home patient who only requires a change of dressings once per day.
- Daily medical office visits conducted and billed for when monthly office visits would be more than adequate.

Medically Unnecessary Services—A service is medically unnecessary and may give rise to a fraudulent scheme when the service is not justified by the patient's medical condition or diagnosis. For example, a claim for payment for an electrocardiogram test may be fraudulent if the patient has no conditions, complaints, or factors which would necessitate the test.

Kickbacks– A health care provider or other person engages in an illegal kickback scheme when he or she offers, solicits, pays, or accepts money, or something of value, in exchange for the referral of a patient for health care services that may be paid for by Medicare or Medicaid. A laboratory owner and doctor each violate the Anti-Kickback statute when the laboratory owner pays the doctor $50 for each Medicare patient a doctor sends to the laboratory for testing. Although kickbacks are often paid in cash based on a percentage of the amount paid by Medicare or Medicaid for a service, kickbacks may take other forms such as jewelry, free paid vacations, or other valuable items.

V. Health Care Fraud Prevention Measures

HCF is not a victimless crime. It increases health care costs for everyone. It is as dangerous as identity theft. Fraud has left many thousands of people injured. Participation in HCF is a crime.

Keeping America's health system free from fraud requires active participation from each of us. The large number of patients, treatments, and complex billing practices attract criminals skilled in victimizing innocent people by committing fraud.

What is Health Care Fraud?

- Altered or fabricated medical bills and other documents.
- Excessive or unnecessary treatments.
- Billing schemes, such as:
    - charging for a service more expensive than the one provided.
    - charging for services that were not provided.
    - duplicate charges.
- False or exaggerated medical disability.
- Collecting on multiple policies for the same illness or injury.

Tips to protect yourself against Health Care Fraud

- Protect your health insurance information card like a credit card.
- Beware of free services--is it too good to be true?
- Review your medical bills, such as your "explanation of benefits," after receiving health care services.
- Check to ensure the dates and services are correct to ensure you get what you paid for.
- If you suspect HCF, call 1-877-327-2583. For more information, visit the web site at http://www.bcbs.com/antifraud.

MORTGAGE FRAUD

I. General Overview

In 2009, the continuing deterioration of the real estate market and the dramatic rise in mortgage delinquencies and foreclosures helped fuel the financial crisis and exposed fraudulent practices that were prevalent throughout the mortgage industry. Weak underwriting standards and unsound risk management practices, which had allowed mortgage fraud perpetrators to exploit lending institutions and avoid detection, became evident once the housing market began declining in 2006.

Mortgage fraud schemes employ some type of material misstatement, misrepresentation, or omission relating to the property or potential borrower which is relied on by an underwriter or lender to fund, purchase, or insure a loan. These misstatements, misrepresentations, or omissions are indicative of mortgage fraud and include the following:

- Inflated Appraisals
- Fictitious/Stolen Identities
- Nominee/Straw Buyers
- False Loan Application
- Fraudulent Supporting Loan Documentation
- Kickbacks

Although there are many different types of schemes, mortgage fraud can be summarized as a form of bank robbery where the bank is not even aware it has been robbed until months or years later. Mortgage fraud perpetrators often obtain loans based on falsely representing the value of the collateral or their qualifications to receive the loan and steal the proceeds without an intention of repaying the borrowed funds. Lending institutions are subsequently left holding the inflated collateral and incurring significant losses.

Mortgage fraud is a part of the FIF subprogram within the FBI's WCCP. The FBI investigates mortgage fraud in two distinct areas: Fraud for Profit, and Fraud for Housing. Those who commit mortgage fraud for profit are often industry insiders using their specialized knowledge or authority to commit or facilitate the fraud. Current investigations and widespread reporting indicate a high percentage of mortgage fraud involves collusion by industry insiders, such as appraisers, mortgage brokers, attorneys, loan originators, and other professionals engaged in the industry. Fraud for Housing typically represents illegal actions conducted solely by the borrower, who is motivated to acquire and maintain ownership of a house under false pretenses such as misrepresented income and asset information on a loan application.

One of the ways the FBI becomes aware of mortgage fraud is through the analysis of Suspicious Activity Reports (SARs), which are filed by federally-insured financial institutions. Mortgage fraud SARs have increased from 6,936 in FY 2003 to 67,190 in FY 2009. These SARs provide valuable intelligence in mortgage fraud trends and can lead to the initiation of mortgage fraud cases, as well as the enhancement of current FBI investigations.

In response to the increase in mortgage fraud, the FBI has continued to add investigative resources to combat the mortgage fraud problem. In December 2008, the FBI dedicated resources to create the NMFT at FBI Headquarters in Washington, D.C. The NMFT has the specific responsibility for all management of the mortgage fraud program at both the origination and corporate level. The NMFT assists the field offices in addressing the mortgage fraud problem at all levels. The current financial crisis, however, has required the FBI to move resources from other WCC and criminal programs in order to appropriately address the crime problem. Since January 2007, the FBI has increased its agent and analyst manpower working mortgage fraud investigations. The NMFT provides tools to identify the most egregious mortgage fraud perpetrators, prioritize pending investigations, and provide information to evaluate where additional manpower is needed.

In September 2009, the FBI established the Financial Intelligence Center (FIC) to provide tactical analysis of intelligence datasets and financial databases. The FIC uses evolving technology and data exploitation techniques to create targeting packages to identify the most egregious criminal enterprises and to enhance current criminal investigations. The FIC has worked jointly with the NMFT to assist the field offices by creating mortgage fraud targeting packages.

One of the best tools the FBI has in its arsenal for combating mortgage fraud is its long-standing partnerships with other federal, state, and local law enforcement. This is not a new tool employed by the FBI. Collaboration, communication, and information sharing have long been a proven solution to the nation's most difficult crimes. In response to a growing gang problem, for example, the FBI formed Safe Streets Task Forces across the country. In response to crimes in Indian Country, the FBI developed the Safe Trails Task Force Program. In response to this new threat, the FBI created Mortgage Fraud Task Forces (MFTF) and Mortgage Fraud Working Groups (MFWG). As of FY 2009, there are 15 MFTFs and 62 MFWGs across the country. With representatives of federal, state, and local law enforcement, these task forces and working groups are strategically placed in locations identified as high-threat areas for mortgage fraud. Partners are varied but typically include representatives of the Federal Deposit Insurance Corporation-OIG, the USPIS, the IRS-CID, FinCEN, and the HUD-OIG, as well as state and local law enforcement officers across the nation.

While the FBI has increased the number of agents around the country who investigate mortgage fraud cases from 120 Special Agents in FY 2007 to 300 Special Agents in FY 2009, this multiagency model serves as a force-multiplier, providing an array of resources to adequately identify the source of the fraud, as well as finding the most effective way to prosecute each case, particularly in active markets where fraud is widespread. We are pleased to report that the model is working.

From the end of January 2009 through October 31, 2009, the FBI and DOJ orchestrated a coordinated mortgage fraud "surge" in the FBI's Jacksonville and Tampa Divisions. The "surge" specifically targeted industry insiders, including loan brokers, lenders, and real estate agents engaged in a variety of mortgage fraud schemes. This effort resulted in charges against more than 100 defendants. The charges involved more than $400 million in loans on more than 700 properties allegedly procured through fraud. This "surge" was launched in response to the epidemic of mortgage fraud throughout the state of Florida. To address this problem, the FBI divisions in both Tampa and Jacksonville, along with the USAO in the Middle District of Florida, began an intensive effort to identify, investigate, and prosecute mortgage fraud in all of its forms. These efforts were led by an FBI MFTF in Florida and involved the cooperation of multiple federal, state, and local law enforcement and governmental agencies.

These valuable partnerships have been instrumental in orchestrating national mortgage fraud takedowns, or "sweeps," during the last few years. By coordinating a number of smaller mortgage fraud cases into a nationwide takedown, the FBI and its partners have been able to raise public awareness of its enforcement efforts and send a strong message aimed at deterring future fraud. These takedowns include Operation Malicious Mortgage in 2008, which resulted in charges against more than 400 defendants in cases across the nation; Operation Quick Flip in 2005, resulting in approximately 156 mortgage fraud defendants; and Operation Continued Action in 2004, which was responsible for initiating more than 150 cases in more than 35 states. Each operation was a success because of the coordination between the FBI and all of its federal, state, and local law enforcement partners.

In addition to the effort placed in creating these task forces and working groups, the FBI is one of the DOJ participants in the national MFWG which meets monthly within Washington, D.C. The national MFWG represents the collaborative effort of multiple federal agencies and facilitates the information-sharing process across the aforementioned agencies, as well as private organizations. Together, we are building on existing FBI intelligence databases to identify large industry insiders and criminal enterprises conducting systemic mortgage fraud.

The FBI has also partnered with a new interagency FFETF to combat financial crime. The FFETF, which is chaired by the Attorney General, is designed to strengthen the collective efforts of federal, state, and local partners to investigate and prosecute significant financial crimes relating to the current financial crisis; to recover ill-gotten gains; and to ensure just and effective punishment for those who perpetrate financial crimes. The mission of the FFETF is not just to hold accountable those who helped bring about the financial meltdown, but to help prevent another meltdown from happening.

In short, the FBI remains committed to its responsibility to aggressively investigate mortgage fraud, as well as engage with the mortgage industry in identifying fraud trends and educating the public. To maximize our current resources, we are relying on intelligence collection and analysis to identify emerging trends and egregious offenders. We will also continue to rely heavily on the strong relationships we have with both our law enforcement and regulatory agency partners to combat mortgage fraud and to target, disrupt, and dismantle the criminal organizations and individuals engaging in these fraud schemes.

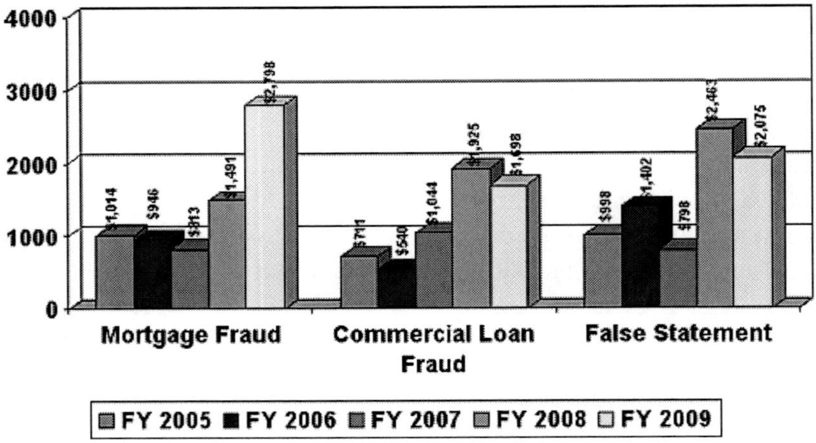

Dollar Losses Reported of Mortgage Related Fraud SARs

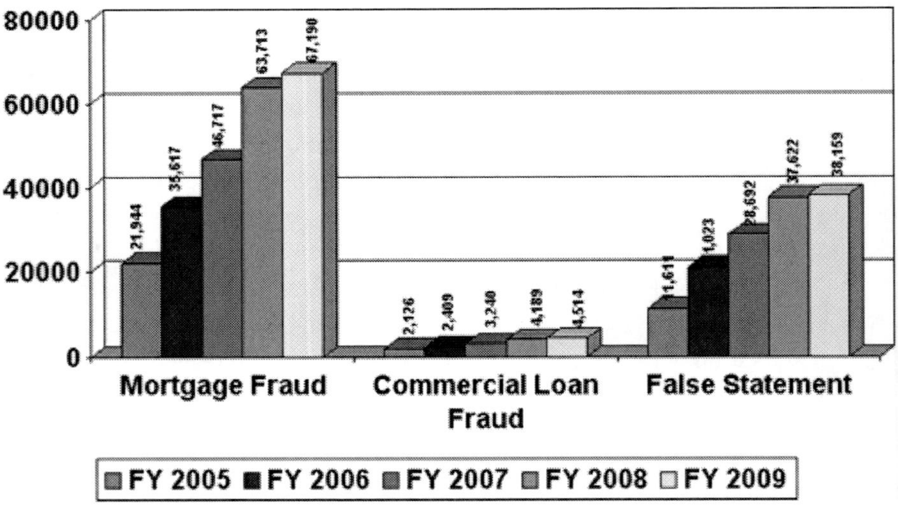

Dollar Losses in Millions
Number of Violations of Mortgage Related Fraud SARs Reported

Regional analysis of SARs containing mortgage fraud violations indicate the Western region of the United States led the nation with 38 percent of mortgage fraud-related SARs filed during FY 2009. Southeastern, North Central, Northeastern, and South Central regions had 28, 17, 11, and 6 percent, respectively, of mortgage fraud-related SAR filings. FBI pending cases indicate the Western region also had the majority of mortgage fraud cases, with 29 percent during 2009. The Southeastern, North Central, Northeastern, and South Central regions had 24, 20, 15, and 12 percent, respectively.

II. Overall Accomplishments

Through FY 2009, 2,794 cases resulted in 822 indictments and 494 convictions of mortgage fraud criminals. The following notable statistical accomplishments are reflective in FY 2009 for mortgage fraud: $2.5 billion in restitutions, $7.5 million in recoveries, and $58.4 million in fines; 128 seizures valued at $5.06 million and 226 criminal indicted assets valued at $510.1 million. The chart below reflects mortgage fraud pending cases from FY 2005 through FY 2009 as follows: FY 2005—721 cases; FY 2006—818 cases; FY 2007—1,204 cases; FY 2008—1,644 cases; and FY 2009—2,794 cases.

III. Significant Cases

Wayne Puff, Affordable Homes Corp. (Newark): From 1998 to 2005, Puff and his coconspirators recruited 1,200 investors from across the country, who poured $123.3 million into New Jersey Affordable Homes Corp. (NJAH). Mr. Puff drew investors by advertising guaranteed annual returns of 15 to 20 percent from his business of buying, renovating, and reselling real estate. The scheme relied on false claims of the company's profits and phony mortgage documents. Puff's co-conspirators included John Kurzel, an NJAH mortgage loan processor, who was sentenced to 20 months in prison; Michael Meehan, a former licensed real estate appraiser, and Anthony Natale, a closing attorney, who were both sentenced to 30 months in prison; Mitchell Fishman, an attorney, and Lucesita Santiago, an NJAH account manager, who were both sentenced to 18 months in prison; and Sydney Raposo, a paralegal for Natale, who was sentenced to six months' home detention. Two defendants are awaiting sentencing. On January 15, 2010, Wayne Puff, the founder of NJAH, a purported real estate investment business, was sentenced to 18 years in prison for defrauding mortgage lenders and investors.

Viktor Kobzar, Kobay Financial (Seattle): Vladislav Baydovskiy, Kobzar and others purchased luxury homes and flipped them to straw buyers, or otherwise unqualified borrowers, using false W-2s, paystubs, bank statements, tax returns, and other fraudulent documents. The loans were brokered through Kobay Financial, which was operated by Baydovskiy and Kobzar. Kobay Financial ceased operations and became Nationwide Home Lending, operated by Alla Sobol, Baydovskiy, and Kobzar. The conspirators closed the loans at Emerald City Escrow, which enabled the subjects to direct loan proceeds to themselves and others. David Sobol (Alla Sobol's husband) and Donata Baydovskiy, aka Netta Brenner (Vladislav Baydovskiy's wife), operated Emerald City Escrow. Brenner and David Sobol assisted in the fraud by preparing double and triple HUD-1 forms to conceal the true loan disbursements and acted as a notary for many transactions. Wade Entezar, a builder, also participated in the fraud scheme. The investigation identified $9 million in loan proceeds diverted to the subjects. Approximately 400 loans were brokered by Kobay/Nationwide, and most are pending review. In addition to Kobzar, Vladislav Baydovskiy, a former mortgage broker, was sentenced to five years in prison; Camie Byron, a loan officer, Alla Sobol, a mortgage broker, and David Sobol, a real estate agent, were each sentenced to two years in prison; Sandra Thorpe, an accountant, was sentenced to probation and 200 hours of community service; and Donata Baydovskiy was sentenced to 265 days in prison and two months of home detention. On January 8, 2010, Victor Kobzar was sentenced to five years in prison for his role as a mortgage broker in a mortgage fraud conspiracy involving at least 68 fraudulent loans resulting in $46 million in loan proceeds.

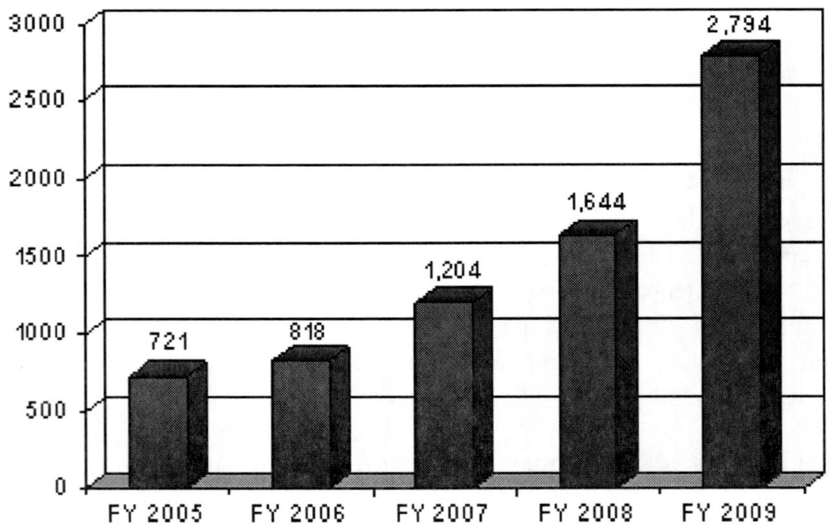

Mortgage Fraud

Robert A. Penn; Stephen S. Brown; Tamara E. Scott (Indianapolis): Between November 2003 and August 2005, Penn, with the aid of Stephen Brown and Tamara Scott, solicited and obtained at least 136 loans from various lenders including Argent Mortgage Company, The MoneyStation, and People's Choice Mortgage/Countrywide Home Loans. Brown was responsible for submitting approximately 43 fraudulent loan applications supported by false documents and inflated appraisals, for which he received between $1,500 and $2,000 per application. Tamara Scott was responsible for attending the mortgage closings, signing fraudulent documents, and receiving checks for loan proceeds. Scott participated in approximately 130 of the fraudulent loans. Brown was sentenced to 37 months in prison and Scott was sentenced to 24 months. In addition, restitution was ordered to be paid by Penn in the amount of $11,411,722; Scott in the amount of $2,793,412; and Brown in the amount of $11,122,891. On January 7, 2010, Robert Penn was sentenced to seven years in prison for his role in brokering approximately $16 million on at least 136 fraudulent mortgages through his various business entities.

IV. Mortgage Fraud Schemes and Trends

Illegal Property Flipping - Property is purchased, falsely appraised at a higher value, and then quickly sold. What makes property flipping illegal is the appraisal information is fraudulent. The schemes typically involve one or more of the following: fraudulent appraisals, falsified loan documentation, inflated buyer income, etc. Kickbacks to buyers, investors, property/loan brokers, appraisers, and title company employees are common in this scheme.

Foreclosure Rescue Schemes—The perpetrators identify homeowners who are in foreclosure or at risk of defaulting on their mortgage loan. The perpetrators then mislead the homeowners into believing they can save their homes by transferring the deed or putting the property in the name of an investor. The perpetrators profit by selling the property to an investor or straw borrower, creating equity using a fraudulent appraisal, and stealing the seller proceeds or fees paid by the homeowners. The homeowners are told they can pay rent for at least a year and repurchase the property once their credit has been reestablished. However, the perpetrators fail to make the mortgage payments and usually the property goes into foreclosure.

Loan Modification Programs—Scammers purport to assist homeowners who are delinquent in their mortgage payments and are on the verge of losing their home by offering to renegotiate the terms of the homeowners' loan with the lender. The scammers, however, demand large fees up-front and often negotiate unfavorable terms for the clients, or do not negotiate at all. Usually, the homeowners ultimately lose their homes. This scheme is similar to a foreclosure rescue scam.

Builder Bailout/Condo Conversion—Builders facing rising inventory and declining demand for newly constructed homes employ bailout schemes to offset losses. Builders find buyers who obtain loans for the properties. The buyers then allow the properties to go into foreclosure. In a condo-conversion scheme, apartment complexes purchased by developers during a housing boom are converted into condos. When the market declines, developers have excess inventory of units. Developers recruit straw buyers with cash-back incentives and inflate the value of the condos to obtain a larger sales price at closing. In addition to failing to disclose the cash-back incentives to the lender, the straw buyers' income and asset information are often inflated in order for them to qualify for properties that they otherwise would be ineligible or unqualified to purchase.

Equity Skimming—An investor may use a straw buyer, false income documents, and false credit reports to obtain a mortgage loan in the straw buyer's name. Subsequent to closing, the straw buyer signs the property over to the investor in a quit claim deed which relinquishes all rights to the property and provides no guaranty to title. The investor does not make any mortgage payments and rents the property until foreclosure takes place several months later.

Silent Second—The buyer of a property borrows the down payment from the seller through the issuance of a nondisclosed second mortgage. The primary lender believes the borrower has invested his own money in the down payment, when in fact, it is borrowed. The second mortgage may not be recorded to further conceal its status from the primary lender.

Home Equity Conversion Mortgage (HECM)- An HECM is a reverse mortgage loan product insured by the Federal Housing Administration (FHA) to borrowers who are 62 years or older, own their own property (or have a small mortgage balance), occupy the property as their primary residence, and participate in HECM counseling. It provides homeowners access to equity in their homes usually in a lump sum payment. Perpetrators recruit seniors through local churches, investment seminars, and television, radio, billboard, and mailer advertisements. The scammers then obtain an HECM in the name of the recruited homeowner to convert equity in the homes into cash. The scammers keep the cash and pay a fee to the senior citizen or take the full amount unbeknownst to the senior citizen. No loan payment or repayment is required until the borrower no longer uses the house as a primary residence. In the scheme, the appraisals on the home are vastly inflated and the lender does not detect the fraud until the homeowner dies and the true value of the property is discovered.

Commercial Real Estate Loans—Owners of distressed commercial real estate obtain financing by creating bogus leases and using these fake leases to exaggerate the building's profitability, thus inflating their appraisal values using the income method approach. These false leases and appraisals trick lenders into extending loans to the owner. As cash flows are restricted to the borrower, property repairs are neglected. By the time the commercial loans are in default, the lender is oftentimes left with dilapidated and unusable or difficult to rent commercial property. Many of the methods of committing mortgage fraud that are found in residential real estate are also present in commercial loan fraud.

Neighborhood Stabilization Program (NSP)—The NSP is a HUD program in which block grants are paid to states, local governments, and nonprofit organizations to encourage the purchase and redevelopment of foreclosed and abandoned properties. Scammers establish nonprofit organizations using shell companies in order to appear qualified to receive grants through the NSP. Additionally, individuals perpetrate traditional loan origination schemes such as false statements and invoices in order to receive funding. Instead of using the funds for redevelopment, the funds are used to enrich the perpetrators.

First-Time Homebuyer Rebate Scheme—Perpetrators take advantage of the American Recovery and Reinvestment Act of 2009 (Stimulus Plan) authorizing a tax credit of up to $8,000 for qualified first-time homebuyers. Subjects create false first-time homebuyer credit claims using the personal information of others, such as relatives or recruited individuals, and receive a check for $8,000 either in the mail or deposited directly into their accounts.

Also, scammers obtain the rebates prior to closing and then cancel the real estate contract.

Air Loans—This is a nonexistent property loan where there is usually no collateral. An example of an air loan would be where a broker invents borrowers and properties, establishes accounts for payments, and maintains custodial accounts for escrows. They may set up an office with a bank of telephones, each one used as the fake employer, appraiser, credit agency, etc., to fraudulently deceive creditors who attempt to verify information on loan applications.

Mortgage Debt Elimination Schemes

- Be aware of e-mails, or web-based advertisements, that promote the elimination of mortgage loans, credit card, and other debts while requesting an up-front fee to prepare documents to satisfy the debt. The documents are typically entitled Declaration of Voidance, Bond for Discharge of Debt, Bill of Exchange, Due Bill, Redemption Certificate, or other similar variations. These documents do not achieve what they purport.
- There is no easy method to relieve your debts.
- Borrowers may end up paying thousands of dollars in fees without the elimination or reduction of any debt.

Foreclosure Fraud Schemes

- Be aware of offers to "save" homeowners who are at risk of defaulting on loans, or whose houses are already in foreclosure.
- Seek a qualified credit counselor or attorney to assist.

Predatory Lending Schemes

- Before purchasing a home, research information about prices of homes in the neighborhood.
- Shop for a lender and compare costs. Beware of lenders who tell you that they are your only chance of getting a loan or owning your own home.

- Beware of "No Money Down" loans. This is a gimmick used to entice consumers to purchase property that they likely cannot afford or are not qualified to purchase. Be wary of mortgage professionals who falsely alter information to qualify the consumer for the loan.
- Do not let anyone convince you to borrow more money than you can afford to repay.
- Do not let anyone persuade you into making a false statement, such as overstating your income, the source of your down payment, or the nature and length of your employment.
- Never sign a blank document or a document containing blanks.
- Read and carefully review all loan documents signed at closing or prior to closing for accuracy, completeness, and omissions.
- Be aware of cost, or loan terms, at closing that are not what you agreed to.
- Do not sign anything you do not understand.
- Be suspicious if the cost of a home improvement goes up in the event you accept the contractor's financing.
- If it sounds too good to be true--it probably is!

Mortgage Fraud Prevention Measures Tips to protect Yourself against Mortgage Fraud

- Get referrals for real estate and mortgage professionals. Check the licenses of the industry professionals with state, county, or city regulatory agencies.
- An outrageous promise of extraordinary profit in a short period of time signals a problem.
- Be wary of strangers and unsolicited contacts, as well as high-pressure sales techniques.
- Look at written information to include recent comparable sales in the area, and other documents such as tax assessments to verify the value of the property.
- Understand what you are signing and agreeing to. If you do not understand, re-read the documents or seek assistance from an attorney or third party.
- Review the title history of the home you are anticipating to purchase to determine if the property has been sold multiple times within a

short period. It could mean that this property has been "flipped," and the value falsely inflated.

- Know and understand the terms of your mortgage. Check your personal information against the information as listed on the loan documents to ensure it is accurate and complete.
- Never sign any loan documents that contain "blanks." This leaves you vulnerable to fraud.
- Check out the tips on the Mortgage Bankers Association's (MBA) website at http://www.StopMortgageFraud.com for additional advice on avoiding Mortgage Fraud.

INSURANCE FRAUD

I. General Overview

Insurance fraud continues to be an investigative priority for the FBI, due in large part to the insurance industry's significant role in the U.S. economy. The U.S. insurance industry consists of thousands of companies and collects nearly $1 trillion in premiums each year. The size of the industry, unfortunately, makes it a prime target for criminal activity; the Coalition Against Insurance Fraud (CAIF) estimates that the cost of fraud in the industry is as high as $80 billion each year. This cost is passed on to consumers in the form of higher premiums. In fact, the NICB calculates that insurance fraud raises the yearly cost of premiums by $300 for the average household.

The downturn in the U.S. economy due to the financial crisis has led to an increase in insurance fraud. The FBI continues to identify the most prevalent schemes and the top echelon criminals defrauding the insurance industry in an effort to reduce insurance fraud. The FBI works closely with the National Association of Insurance Commissioners, NICB, CAIF, as well as state fraud bureaus, state insurance regulators, and other federal agencies to combat Insurance Fraud. In addition, the FBI is a member of the International Association of Insurance Fraud Agencies, an international nonprofit organization whose mission is to maintain an international presence to address insurance and insurance-related financial crimes on a global basis. Currently, the FBI is focusing a majority of its resources relating to insurance fraud on the following schemes:

Insurance-Related Corporate Fraud—Although corporate fraud is not unique to any particular industry, there have been instances involving insurance companies caught in the web of these schemes. The temptations for fraud within the corporate industry can be greater during periods of financial downturns. Insurance companies hold customer premiums which are forbidden from operational use by the company. However, when funding is needed, unscrupulous executives invade the premium accounts in order to pay corporate expenses. This leads to financial statement fraud because the company is required to "cover its tracks" to conceal the improper utilization of customer premium funds.

Premium Diversion/Unauthorized Entities- The most common type of fraud involves insurance agents and brokers diverting policyholder premiums for their own benefit. Additionally, there are a growing number of unauthorized and unregistered entities engaged in the sale of insurance-related products. As the insurance industry becomes open to foreign players, regulation becomes more difficult. Additionally, exponentially rising insurance costs in certain areas (i.e., terrorism insurance, directors'/officers' insurance, and corporations), increase the possibility for this type of fraud.

Viatical Settlement Fraud- A viatical settlement is a discounted, pre-death sale of an existing life insurance policy on the life of a person known to have a terminal condition. The parties to a viatical settlement include the insured party, insurance agent/broker, insurance company, viatical company/broker, and the investor. Viatical settlement fraud occurs when misrepresentations are made on the insurance policy applications, in effect, hiding the fact that the party applying for a policy has already been diagnosed with a terminal condition. On the investor end, the fraud occurs when misrepresentations are made to the investors by the viatical companies about life expectancies of insured parties and guaranteed high rates of return.

Workers' Compensation Fraud—The Professional Employer Organization (PEO) industry operates chiefly to provide workers' compensation insurance coverage to small businesses by pooling businesses together to obtain reasonable rates. Workers' compensation insurance accounts for as much as 46 percent of small business owners' general operating expenses. Due to this, small business owners have an incentive to shop workers' compensation insurance on a regular basis. This has made it ripe for entities that purport to provide workers' compensation insurance to enter the marketplace, offer reduced premium rates, and misappropriate funds without providing insurance. The focus of these investigations is on allegations that numerous entities within the PEO industry are selling unauthorized and non-admitted workers' compensation coverage to businesses across the United States. This insurance fraud scheme has left injured and deceased victims without workers' compensation coverage to pay their medical bills.

With the cooperation of the insurance industry, through referrals from industry liaison and other law enforcement agencies, the FBI continues to target the individuals and organizations committing insurance fraud. The FBI continues to initiate and conduct traditional investigations as well as utilize sophisticated techniques, to include undercover investigations, to apprehend the fraudsters.

Disaster Fraud— When a disaster occurs, there are many organizations and individuals soliciting contributions for the victims of this disaster. Most of the organizations and individuals involved are legitimate; however, there are some who are not. Victims may be approached by unsolicited e-mails asking for donations to a legitimate-sounding organization. The schemer will instruct the victim to send a donation via a money transfer. Other types of disaster fraud include false or exaggerated claims by policyholders; misclassification of flood damage as wind, fire, or theft; claims filed by individuals residing hundreds of miles outside the disaster zone; bid-rigging by contractors; falsely inflating the cost of repairs; and contractors requiring up-front payment for services, then failing to perform the agreed upon repairs.

Staged Auto Accidents—Perpetrators of staged auto accidents will either stage an accident with coconspirators, or maneuver innocent motorists into accidents. Although the resulting property damage may be small, the perpetrators make large—and illegal— claims for fake injuries and property damage. This type of fraud results in higher insurance premiums for all drivers.

Property Insurance Fraud—Perpetrators of property insurance fraud seek to obtain payment that is higher than the value of the property damaged or destroyed, or intentionally destroy property that could not be sold. Common examples include arson, scuttling of boats, and the ditching of vehicles in lakes or canals.

II. Overall Accomplishments

During FY 2009, 152 cases investigated by the FBI resulted in 43 indictments/informations, 22 arrests, and 42 convictions of insurance fraud criminals. The following notable statistical accomplishments reflect FY 2009 for insurance fraud: $22.9 million in restitutions and $31.4 million in recoveries and $618,480 in seizures. The following reflects insurance fraud pending cases from FY 2005 through FY 2009 as follows: FY 2005—270 cases; FY 2006—233 cases; FY 2007—209 cases; FY 2008 -177 cases; and FY 2009 —152 cases. Although the FBI has focused its efforts on higher priority WCC matters, insurance fraud investigations continue to be addressed utilizing liaison efforts in conjunction with other federal, state, and local law enforcement.

III. Significant Case

John Wayne Goff, dba The Goff Group (Birmingham): On June 2, 2009, a former insurance executive who was convicted of mail fraud, embezzlement, and filing a false report with the state insurance department was sentenced to 12 years in prison. The executive was the former owner of a company that collected workers' compensation premiums for insurance companies. The executive willfully failed to remit to the insurance companies their fair share of the premiums. The executive unlawfully and illegally withheld approximately $3 million in premiums. The executive instead spent the money for his own personal expenditures, including an exorbitant salary, lavish lifestyle, corporate aircraft, and real estate investments. He was indicted on April 2, 2008, for 26 counts of mail fraud, embezzlement of insurance company funds, conspiracy, and false statements to a state department of insurance. He was convicted on February 18, 2009, on 23 counts of mail fraud, false statements to the state department of insurance, and embezzlement.

MASS MARKETING FRAUD

I. General Overview

Mass marketing fraud is a general term for frauds which exploit mass-communication media, such as telemarketing, mass mailings, and the Internet. Since the 1930s, mass marketing has been a widely accepted and exercised practice. Advances in telecommunications and financial services technologies have further served to spur growth in mass marketing, both for legitimate business purposes, as well as for the perpetration of consumer frauds.

While these fraud schemes may take a wide variety of forms, they share a common theme: the use of false and/or deceptive representations to induce potential victims to make advance fee-type payments to fraud perpetrators. Although there are no comprehensive statistics on the subject, it is estimated mass marketing frauds victimize millions of Americans each year and generate losses in the hundreds of millions of dollars. The following is a brief description of some of the key concepts and schemes associated with the mass marketing/ advance fee fraud crime problem.

Advance Fee Fraud—This category of fraud encompasses a broad variety of schemes which are designed to induce their victims into remitting up-front payments in exchange for the promise of goods, services, and/or prizes. Some of the most prevalent schemes being encountered are the following:

Nigerian Letter Fraud—Victims are contacted regarding substantial sums of money held in foreign accounts and are requested to pay various fees to secure their transfer to the United States, in exchange for a portion of the total proceeds. Alternatively, victims are asked to act as a U.S. agent in securing the release of such funds and are provided with counterfeit instruments which are to be cashed in order to pay any required fees, only to discover they must reimburse their financial institution for cashing a counterfeit instrument. A variation of this fraud involves the use of fraudulent websites, which have been created to resemble website pages of legitimate financial institutions, to enhance the scheme's credibility and swindle greater amounts of money from victims. The victims are directed to open accounts at the fictitious banks' websites into which the perpetrators transfer the victims' funds. Victims cannot withdraw or transfer the funds when they log onto the fictitious bank websites and are prompted to pay additional taxes or fees before the funds can be released. The funds are never released.

Foreign Lottery/Sweepstakes Fraud—Victims are informed they have won a substantial prize in a foreign drawing, but must remit payment for various taxes/fees to receive their winnings.

Alternatively, victims are provided with counterfeit instruments, representing a portion of the winnings, which are to be cashed in order to pay the required fees, only to discover they must reimburse their financial institution for cashing a counterfeit instrument.

Overpayment Fraud—Victims who have advertised some item for sale are contacted by buyers who remit counterfeit instruments, in excess of the purchase price, for payment. The victims are told to cash the payments, deduct any expenses, and return or forward the excess funds to an individual identified by the buyer, only to discover they must reimburse their financial institution for cashing a counterfeit instrument.

Recovery Schemes—Victims are contacted by perpetrators posing as law enforcement officers, government employees, or lawyers to inform victims that the persons responsible for the original fraud schemes have been arrested or successfully sued and their bank accounts have been seized. The victims are told the seized money is going to be returned to the victims, but the victims must first pay fees for processing and administrative services. Recovery pitches often target victims many months or years after the original fraud schemes.

The predominantly transnational nature of the mass marketing fraud crime problem presents significant impediments to effective investigation by any single agency or national jurisdiction. Typically, victims will reside in one or more countries, perpetrators will operate from another, and the financial/money services infrastructure of numerous additional countries are utilized for the rapid movement and laundering of funds. For these reasons, the FBI is uniquely positioned to assist in the investigation of these frauds through its network of Legal Attache (Legat) Offices located in over 60 U.S. embassies around the world. By leveraging its global presence and network of liaison contacts, the FBI has successfully cooperated with other domestic and foreign law enforcement agencies to combat, disrupt, and dismantle international Mass Marketing Fraud groups. The FBI participates in the International Mass Marketing Fraud Working Group (IMMFWG), a multiagency working group established to facilitate the multinational exchange of information and intelligence, the coordination of cross-border operational matters, and the enhancement of public awareness of international mass marketing fraud schemes. The current membership of the IMMFWG consists of law enforcement, regulatory, and consumer protection agencies from seven countries, including Australia, Belgium, Canada, the Netherlands, Nigeria, the United Kingdom, and the United States.

Despite the best interagency enforcement efforts to combat mass marketing fraud, the FBI remains cognizant of the fact the only enduring remedy for this crime problem lies in consumer education and fraud prevention programs. Towards this end, the FBI has not only produced its own mass marketing fraud prevention pamphlet, but coordinates on other public information efforts with the DOJ, FTC, and the USPIS. The FBI also supports a consumer fraud prevention website in conjunction with the USPIS which can be located on the web at:

II. Overall Accomplishments

As of the end of FY 2009, the FBI was investigating 89 cases of mass marketing fraud and had already recorded multiple indictments and convictions. The following reflects mass marketing fraud pending cases from FY 2005 through FY 2009 as follows: FY 2005—161 cases; FY 2006—147 cases; FY 2007—127 cases; FY 2008—100 cases; and FY 2009—89 cases. Although the FBI has focused its efforts on higher priority WCC matters, mass marketing fraud investigations continue to be addressed utilizing liaison efforts in conjunction with other federal, state, and local law enforcement agencies and the IMMFWG.

III. Significant Cases

Israeli-Based Telemarketing Fraud (New York): This investigation centered on the activities of an Israeli-based boiler room. The perpetrators, all residents of Israel, contacted hundreds of elderly victims in the United States to inform them they had won substantial cash prizes in an international sweepstakes lottery, but in order to claim these prizes, they first needed to pay several thousand dollars in fees. Victims who had already sent money were often contacted again by the managers to send additional money in order to claim their prizes. The total fraud proceeds are estimated to be in excess of $2 million. During 2009, a total of eight subjects were arrested as a result of this investigation. This investigation was worked by FBI New York, in cooperation with the Tel Aviv Fraud Division of the Israel National Police. This case involves the largest number of Israeli citizens ever to be provisionally arrested by Israel in anticipation of extradition.

Vancouver-Based Telemarketing Fraud (Los Angeles): This investigation centered on the activities of a Vancouver-based fraudulent telemarketing and money transfer operation. The perpetrators, residents of Vancouver, British Columbia, mailed letters to thousands of elderly U.S. victims that falsely represented they were winners of a monetary prize, such as a lottery or sweepstakes. Included with the letters was a fraudulent check, which the perpetrators claimed was sent to help them pay some required fees. The victims were instructed to utilize a money transfer service, such as MoneyGram, to pay these fees. Many victims wired these fees before realizing that the checks they received were fraudulent. As a result of this scheme, victims lost in excess of $10 million in money transfer payments. During 2009, two subjects were arrested as a result of this investigation.

This investigation was worked by FBI Los Angeles, in cooperation with the Royal Canadian Mounted Police Project Emptor Task Force, the USPIS, and FTC.

Tips to Protect Yourself Against Mass Marketing Fraud

Things you should do:

- Insist on learning the full name, address, and contact information for any company soliciting your business, personal information, or assistance.
- Insist that all solicitors send materials to you in writing so that you are able to study the full details of the offer, as well as any guarantees, and/or refund policies.

- Research all solicitors through the Better Business Bureau, state Attorney General's Office, and/or consumer protection service in the state or city where the company is located.
- Prior to making any significant financial decisions, consult a family member, friend, your attorney, accountant, and/or other trusted advisor for an objective opinion.
- To stop receiving telephone solicitations, instruct solicitors to delete your contact information from all call lists and register with the FTC's "Do Not Call" Registry.
- Report suspicious telemarketing calls, mail solicitations, or advertisements to the FTC at 1-877-FTC-HELP or online at http://www.ftc.gov.

Things you should NOT do:

- Do not make any payments to either secure a prize or improve your chances of winning a prize.
- Do not be intimidated into making hasty financial decisions by high-pressure sales tactics.
- Do not provide anyone with your sensitive personal or financial information unless:
  a) it is to an entity whose legitimacy is personally known to you, and
  b) you personally initiated the contact with the entity.
- Do not send funds via wire or electronic money transfer services unless:
  a) it is to an entity whose legitimacy is personally known to you, and
  b) you personally initiated the contact with the entity.
- Do not be lured by offers that are simply too good to be true...they almost certainly are.

ASSET FORFEITURE/MONEY LAUNDERING

I. General Overview

The mission of the AF/MLU is to promote the strategic use of the asset forfeiture and to ensure field offices employ the money laundering violation in all investigations, where appropriate, to disrupt and/or dismantle criminal enterprises. The asset forfeiture and money laundering process identifies targets, disrupts, and dismantles criminal and terrorist organizations and individuals engaged in fraud schemes which target our nation's financial infrastructure.

The implementation of the asset forfeiture process to criminal investigation provides law enforcement with opportunity to remove the tools of crime from criminal organizations, deprives wrongdoers of the proceeds of their crimes, recovers property that may be used to compensate victims, and deters crimes. The asset forfeiture process can destroy the financial infrastructure of criminal enterprises, return funds to victims of large-scale fraud, and share forfeiture property with state and local law enforcement agencies.

The AF Program and the ML Program provide support to all FBI investigative programs, to include International and Domestic Terrorism.

MONEY LAUNDERING

The DOJ defines money laundering in the following manner:

"Money laundering is the process by which criminals conceal or disguise the proceeds of their crimes or convert those proceeds into goods and services. It allows criminals to infuse their illegal money into the stream of commerce, thus corrupting financial institutions and the money supply, thereby giving criminal's unwarranted economic power."

The FBI maintains a proactive approach when investigating money laundering. After identifying a Specified Unlawful Activity that generates illicit proceeds, a parallel financial investigation is conducted in order to locate the proceeds and prove their connection to the underlying crime.

Asset Forfeiture

The FBI's AF Program is one of the most successful in all of law enforcement. In the WCCP, the bulk of the monies seized are returned to victims of the frauds that generated them. This is unique to the FBI and some other agencies. Most people associate the seizure and forfeiture of assets with narcotics trafficking. Although the FBI does seize assets from drug dealers and other criminals, the WCCP is the largest contributor to the FBI's forfeiture program.

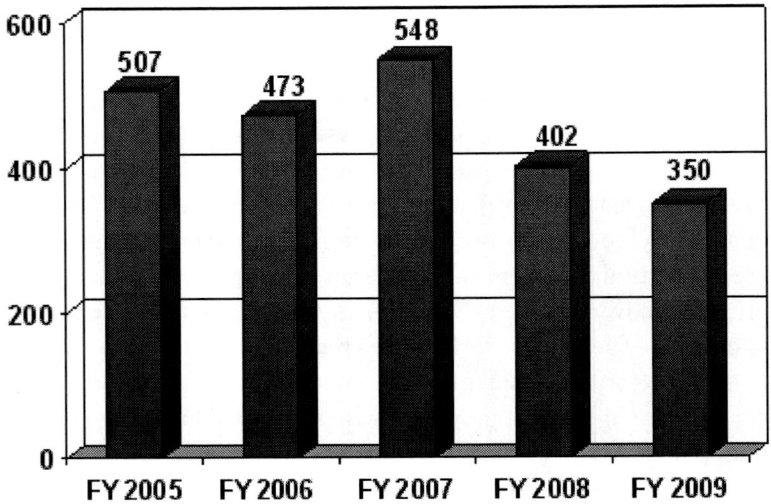

Money Laundering Pending Cases

II. Overall Accomplishments

Through FY 2009, 350 cases investigated by the FBI resulted in 43 indictments and 84 convictions of ML fraud criminals. For FY 2009, the following ML most notable accomplishments were achieved for the WCCP: $81.9 million in restitutions, $643,000 in recoveries, and $1.5 million in fines. The chart below reflects ML pending cases from FY 2005 through FY 2009 as follows: FY 2005—507 cases; FY 2006— 473 cases; FY 2007—548 cases; FY 2008—402 cases; and FY 2009—350 cases.

III. Significant Cases

Cashtrica (New York): FBI New York Agents participated in a joint investigation with Rockland County, NY, law enforcement, targeting La Cosa Nostra (LCN) subjects that were running a multimillion-dollar Internet gambling operation out of Costa Rica. Based on experience garnered in that investigation, agents formulated a plan to attack the entire internet gambling industry by targeting all facets to include; online gaming companies, banks, money transfer businesses, and the owners of same. Significant targets included: Neteller PLC, Partygaming PLC, Sportingbet PLC, Fireone Group

PLC, HSBC, Dresdner Bank, and Canaccord Capital, to name a few. As a result of investigation to date, the targets listed above, as well as several others, are fully cooperating with the FBI. Key cooperators have recently been tasked to identify companies, individuals, assets, and to conduct consensual recordings. Liaison with Legats in Canada, Europe, South America, and the Bahamas has been necessary to the success of this ongoing investigation into what has become a virtually worldwide criminal industry. This investigation thus far has obtained evidence of money laundering, mail fraud, wire fraud, bank fraud, securities fraud, credit card fraud, and illegal gambling. There has also been clear indication of an expertise in moving vast sums of money around the world while effectively masking the associated transactions. Forfeiture to date: $364,265,995.86.

Hassan Nemazee (New York): Hassan Nemazee is a multimillionaire Iranian-American investment banker. Nemazee is one of the top political donors in the United States. Nemazee obtained approximately $230,000,000 in loans from Bank of America (BoA), HSBC, and other banks. It was determined that the collateral securing the loans was based on false and misleading information. Nemazee was arrested as he was attempting to flee to Italy. A meeting was held with Daylight FAs, retained by BoA to trace the flow of illegal proceeds. Numerous seizure warrants were executed against various accounts owned/controlled by Nemazee. Having learned that they were in possession of illegal proceeds, Citibank wired $75,000,000 to the U.S. Marshals Asset Forfeiture Account for forfeiture. Plea negotiations with Nemazee's partner are continuing, which could lead to the receipt of another $40 million.

Bernard Madoff (New York): On December 10, 2008, Bernard L. Madoff was arrested for perpetrating the largest Ponzi scheme in history, $64 billion, through the Madoff Investment Advisory (MIA). The fraud involved thousands of victims and numerous targets. The Madoff office space contained approximately 3,000 banking boxes of potential evidence; additionally, a warehouse contained approximately 9,000 more banking boxes of evidence. Madoff conspired with two computer programmers who created a proprietary software system which was used to document false trades and issue bogus statements. The system was the foundation for the Ponzi scheme. The fraudulent documents were so effective the fraud went on for decades and cleared audits by the SEC as well as major financial institutions. Various institutions and individual funds invested their clients' funds into the Madoff

Ponzi scheme. These entities are referred to as "feeder funds" because they "fed" the MIA Ponzi fraud. Without this consistent injection of capital the fraud could not have been maintained for the length of time that it was. As many as 50 funds fed the MIA. Many of the feeder fund managers appear to have been excessively compensated. Finally, Madoff used an elaborate flow of funds from domestic banks to offshore banks to cloak the fraudulent activity in the MIA.

FORENSIC ACCOUNTANT PROGRAM

I. General Overview

In March 2009, the FBI created the Forensic Accountant Program (FAP) and instituted the Forensic Accountant Unit (FAU) within the CID, FCS. The Forensic Accountant position was developed in an effort to attract and retain top-tier accounting professionals who possess the ability to conduct complex, thorough forensic financial investigations.

The FAP is the culmination of years of effort to advance and professionalize the FBI's financial investigative capabilities. The FBI's FoAs will be expected to testify as expert witnesses in judicial proceedings and essentially retain ownership of the financial investigative portion of complex investigations with little guidance from the respective Case Agent(s).

The mission of the FAU is to support all FBI investigative matters requiring a forensic financial investigation and to ensure the FBI's financial investigative priorities are continually addressed. The FAU seeks to provide the highest caliber of financial investigative work-product and support as well as contributing to the FBI's Intelligence Cycle. The FAU is developing and implementing a rigorous training curriculum and partnering with an array of public and private organizations in an effort to cultivate a workforce that provides superior results both in the field offices and at FBIHQ.

II. Initiatives

Forensic Accountant Core Training Session Training Course

In FY 2009, the FAU initiated development of a rigorous training curriculum titled the Forensic Accountant Core Training Session ("FACTS").

FACTS is a comprehensive introductory program of instruction designed to increase an FoA's proficiency in the critical areas necessary to conduct a financial investigation. This extensive course will develop the FoAs aptitude and knowledge in handling a financial investigation according to pertinent rules and regulations across a wide variety of subject matters. The FAU developed the FACTS training curriculum and will be responsible for administering the training. The material covered will focus primarily on providing an overview of FBI programs and systems, financial investigative topics and techniques, resources available to develop an investigation, legal training, and expert witness-testifying techniques.

BankScan Initiative

BankScan is an in-house-created software application which translates physical bank and credit card statements into an electronic medium, thus dramatically decreasing the time-consuming data-entry process. In FY 2009, FAU deployed the BankScan training initiative, "Train the Trainer" with the goal of full field office deployment by the end of FY 2010. The Train the Trainer Initiative was completed, and each field office "Trainer" received the requisite training and was supplied with the necessary software and equipment to implement the BankScan Project. Since its implementation, the FBI has benefited through an exponential increase in financial investigative efficiency and productivity.

Electronic Subpoena Production

The Electronic Subpoena Production initiative represents a joint undertaking of the FBI's CID, DOJ's Criminal Division Fraud Section, and the IRS. Electronic Subpoena Production requires financial institutions to digitally produce account data stored electronically by relying on existing Rule 17 of the Federal Rules of Criminal Procedure. When used in conjunction with BankScan, the introduction of this new process will substantially increase the efficiency and effectiveness of FBI forensic financial investigations.

Financial Analyst Conversion

In FY 2009, the FAU developed a selective conversion process to transition qualified FAs to the FoAP to provide the FBI's investigative programs with the highest caliber of financial investigative work-product and support. This effort will ensure only those individuals who meet the FoA requirements are selectively converted to the FoAP.

III. Significant Cases

The FAU has provided substantial support to major cases such as the Madoff, Stanford, and Bad Medicine (health care fraud) investigations.

Madoff Investigation: The FAU provided substantial support to the New York Field Office to address the Madoff investigation. The FAU coordinated with several field offices to provide three Forensic Accountants, equipment, and resources to support this investigation over a five-month period. The critical work performed by the FoAs significantly advanced the investigation and the respective statistical accomplishments.

Stanford Financial Group: The FAU supported Houston Field Office by providing an FA to support the Stanford Financial Group investigation. This $7 billion Ponzi scheme has resulted in numerous indictments and guilty pleas. The financial investigation performed by the FA was a key contribution in furthering this investigation.

Bad Medicine: The FAU coordinated with multiple field offices to provide three FAs to expedite this financial investigation. To date, 168 indictments charging 107 individuals have been returned. The forensic financial analysis performed by the FAs was critical to the investigation and the resulting indictments.

Scott Rothstein: The FAU augmented the Miami Field Office providing Forensic Accountants and FAs in the ongoing Scott Rothstein financial investigation. The investigation into this $1 billion Ponzi scheme was advanced by the contributions of the FAs and FoAs and contributed to the five-count indictment and the subsequent guilty plea entered by the defendant.

Acronyms

AF/MLU	Asset Forfeiture/Money Laundering Unit
BCBSA	Blue Cross and Blue Shield Association
BLMIS	Bernard L. Madoff Investment Services, LLC
BoA	Bank of America
CAIF	Coalition Against Insurance Fraud

CFO	Chief Financial Officer
CFTC	Commodities Futures Trading Commission
CID	Criminal Investigative Division
CMS	Centers for Medicare and Medicaid Services
DBA	Doing Business As
DEA	Drug Enforcement Administration
DME	Durable Medical Equipment
DOJ	Department of Justice
EBRI	Electronic Bank Records Initiative
ECU	Economic Crimes Unit
FA	Financial Analyst
FACTS	Forensic Accountant Core Training Session
FAP	Forensic Accountant Program
FAU	Forensic Accountant Unit
FBI	Federal Bureau of Investigation
FCIU	Financial Crimes Intelligence Unit
FCS	Financial Crimes Section
FDA	Food and Drug Administration
FFETF	Financial Fraud Enforcement Task Force
FHA	Federal Housing Administration
FIC	Financial Intelligence Center
FIF	Financial Institution Fraud
FIFU	Financial Institution Fraud Unit
FinCEN	Financial Crimes Enforcement Network
FINRA	Financial Industry Regulation Authority
FoA	Forensic Accountant
FSP	Forfeiture Support Project
FTC	Federal Trade Commission
FY	Fiscal Year
GDP	Gross Domestic Product
HCF	Health Care Fraud
HCFU	Health Care Fraud Unit
HECM	Home Equity Conversion Mortgage
HHA	Home Health Agency
HHCFI	Home Health Care Fraud Initiative
HHS	Health and Human Services
HUD	Housing and Urban Development
HYIF	High Yield Investment Fraud
ICE	Immigration and Customs Enforcement

IMMFWG	International Mass Marketing Fraud Working Group
IPofA	Investment Properties of America
IRS	Internal Revenue Service
LCN	La Cosa Nostra
LEGAT	Legal Attache
MBA	Mortgage Bankers Association
MFTF	Mortgage Fraud Task Force
MFWG	Mortgage Fraud Working Group
MIA	Madoff Investment Advisory
NJAH	New Jersey Affordable Homes
NMFT	National Mortgage Fraud Team
NHCAA	National Health Care Anti-Fraud Association
NICB	National Insurance Crime Bureau
NSP	Neighborhood Stabilization Program
OIG	Office of Inspector General
PEO	Professional Employer Organization
SAR	Suspicious Activity Reports
SEC	Securities and Exchange Commission
SIGTARP	Special Inspector General for the Trouble Asset Relief Program
STM	ST Microelectronics
USAO	U.S. Attorney's Office
USPIS	U.S. Postal Inspection Service
WCC	White Collar Crime
WCCP	White Collar Crime Program

CHAPTER SOURCES

The following chapters have been previously published:

Chapter 1 – This is an edited, excerpted and augmented edition of a United States Congressional Research Service publication, Report Order Code RL34603, dated December 16, 2009.

Chapter 2 – This is an edited, excerpted and augmented edition of a United States Congressional Research Service publication, Report Order Code RS22594, dated February 2, 2007.

Chapter 3 – This is an edited, excerpted and augmented edition of a United States Congressional Reference Service publication.

Chapter 4 – This is an edited, excerpted and augmented edition of a United States Congressional Reference Service Summary, dated 2009.

Chapter 5 – This is an edited, excerpted and augmented edition of a Federal Crimes Section (part of the Federal Bureau of Investigation) publication, dated Fiscal Year 2009. (October 1, 2008-September 30, 2009)

Index

C

D

E

F

U

V

W